Lazy Traveler's City Walk

Lazy Traveler's City Walk

Armchair travelers walking optional

Sitansu Ghosh

Lekhoni Publisher

Lazy Traveler's City Walk by Sitansu Ghosh

Disclaimer
The writings in this book are stories based on the author's observation, the travel guide's narration, promotional materials, and online sources. The purpose of these stories is enjoyment and inspiration.

Published by Lekhoni Publisher
2613 Crossvine Drive
Dumfries, VA

Copyright © 2023 by Sitansu Ghosh
All rights reserved. This book or any portion thereof may not be reproduced or used in any manner without the publisher's express written permission, except for using brief quotations in a book review.

Paperback ISBN: 9798362788964

Printed in the United States of America
First Printing, 2023
Lekhoni Publisher
2613 Crossvine Drive
Dumfries, VA 22026
101548trader@gmail.com

Printed in the United States
First paperback Edition September 2023

Published by Lekhoni Publisher
2613 Crossvine Drive
Dumfries, VA 22026
101548trader@gmail.com

Acknowledgment

I sincerely thank my wife for encouraging me and putting up with my disappearing in my home office. She has read my book and suggested improvements and corrections. She has helped me with the design of the book cover. This book would not have been possible without her patience and perseverance.

Thanks to my editors David Drum, Yougadhish Das, Shesh Srivatsa, Sukti Ghosh, Sumita Gupta, and Aloka Dalal. My editors read through my work, corrected any errors, commented, and suggested improvements.

I also thank Milton Biswas and Rajat Ray for their help capturing beautiful photos from faraway cities.

Finally, thanks to all my relatives and friends who encouraged me, listened to my stories, and expressed interest in reading the book when it is published.

Forward

This is a book of travel stories. This is not a traditional travel book. There is no guidance, directions, or reviews. There is no arrival and getting around chapter. There are excellent books for helping a traveler go to a place and enjoy the best available.

This book tells interesting, unusual, and not-so-hidden stories from world cities. The Lazy Traveler picks up these stories while walking the cities of London and New Castle upon Tyne in England, Barcelona in Spain, Kolkata in India, Verona in Italy, and Montpelier in the United States.

The author attempted to bring the readers the joy of discovery and serendipities. The author's love of photography helped him present his stories with beautiful photographs.

As he travels from one country to another and to new cities, he marvels at unexpected discoveries. Calcutta Becomes Kolkata is a story of Calcutta's transformation into a modern-day metropolis. Barcelona - the Street Lamp opened a door into the Spanish culture of siesta. William Shakespeare's play Romeo and Juliet came alive in the Juliet of Verona story. Torture in the Tower is a funny story of hunts for a Mughal diamond in the Tower of London. Dabbawal upon Tyne is a tale of two cities, Mumbai, India, and New Castle upon Tyne, England. Roadometer to Odometer opened the history of an invention and the emigration of the pioneers along the Oregon and California trail.

The lazy traveler traveled in big buses with expert drivers and capable tour managers. The bus becomes the home and community for the forty or so travelers. Avoiding preflight delays, long security lines, and post-flight delays for baggage or the disaster of lost luggage is almost impossible. However, once on the bus, it is time to be lazy.

The stories in this book may bring your own travel ideas and inspire you to step onto a bus. Or you may sit on an armchair to enjoy the stories and the photographs – walking is optional.

Table of Content

Copyright
Acknowledgment
Forward

Calcutta Becomes Kolkata

Barcelona - the Street Lamp

Juliet of Verona

Torture at the Tower

Dabbawal upon Tyne

Roadometer to Odometer

Calcutta becomes Kolkata

Calcutta is a fascinating city. Every Bengali knows that, and every Bengali has a story. I have my own account: the mystery city of my childhood. Calcutta was the capital of British India. Later it became the capital of the State of West Bengal. Calcutta was big – huge. All over West Bengal, there were many big and small towns; however, none came close in size to Calcutta. Wide paved roads with public transportation, like trams, buses, and taxis, existed only in Calcutta. Multi-storied buildings lined up on both sides of the city streets. This city was the home of dazzling movie theaters and historic buildings. Numerous markets, shops, and vendors were selling all kinds of merchandise throughout the city all day.

In 1772, the first Governor-General of British India, Warren Hastings, made Calcutta the capital of British India. Calcutta was the capital until 1911. In that year, Delhi replaced Calcutta as the capital of India. There are many reasons for the Bengalis to be proud of the city. Like the General Post Office, the building was the first of its kind in India. Many other firsts in India in Calcutta were the printing press and newspaper, banks, telegraph lines, tram car service, the introduction of electricity, and the first metro train system in modern India. Above all, the city was a hotbed of armed resistance and non-violent independence movements against British Rule. Calcutta did not lack any international reputation. Rabindranath Tagore, born and raised in Calcutta, was the first Indian to receive the Nobel Prize for literature in 1913. Mother Teresa created the

Top   Tram in Calcutta

Left   General Post Office

Missionaries of Charity in Calcutta. She received Nobel Prize for Peace in 1979.

Growing up in a small town about sixty miles north of Calcutta, visiting the city was a special treat. In fact, there were only a few such treats when I was in school. During those visits, I lived with my aunt and cousins in a flat (apartment) on Mirzapur Street. This street was in the northern part of the city near Sealdah station.

I liked the small crowded apartment only in the early mornings. I would get up early and sit on the gari baranda, a veranda overhanging the Mirzapur Street footpath (sidewalk). I watched the streets in the mixed light. The streetlights were still on, and soft light was coming from the rising sun just above the horizon. I could see almost up to Harrison Road on my left, east, and College Street to Central Avenue on my right, west. Mirzapur Street was very busy. It connected three busy city highways running north and south through the city. All kinds of traffic flowed all day – yellow top taxis, private autos, hand-pulled rickshaws, motorcycles, and bikes. Vendors set up their temporary stalls on sidewalks on both sides of the street. They were selling street food, raw vegetables, cooking utensils, and many other commodities and services, including the services of a priest and a fortune-teller. The priest would walk to the storekeepers and vendors on the sidewalk each morning and perform Pooja for them. The street was

Below Calcutta Gariahat, Intersection of Gariahat Road and Rash Behari Avenue. Jashdha Bhavan – The iconic Gariahat Building at the intersection.

Right Calcutta Double decker bus, Calcutta State Transport Corporation Maniktala Bus Depot,

noisy all day, with vehicle horns, vendors shouting their products, and people walking and talking.

In the early morning, the street below was quiet. I could hear the clunking sound of the trams passing on College Street. Then, in between clunks, the sounds of stick brooms sweeping began and grew louder. The Jharudar, a city sweeper with a broom, went into action. The street sweeping, followed by washing the street with water from hoses.

By that time, the newspaper delivery person, on a bike, was tossing papers toward the porches, verandas, windows, doors, and any place where a rolled-up newspaper could rest. A little boy, younger than me, fired the tea stall's big open coal-burning stove across the road. Just around that time, the Ganga maatee salesperson would go past the street below with a bamboo basket full of chunks of his commodity. Ganga maatee was clay collected from the banks of the river Ganges. This clay is considered holy and used in religious rituals. It is also used for applying lining to coal-fired, small stoves. At that time gas fired cooking stoves were rare in Calcutta. Why on earth would anybody spend money to buy Ganga maatee?

The river Ganges was about one and a half miles from our home, and we could get tons of clay free of charge. We could just dig it up and carry it home on our bikes. My aunt explained that nobody had time to go to the river and get clay in Calcutta. In addition, there was the convenience of city living. She told me that if I paid, I could get whatever I needed by just sitting on my front porch. For the next few days, I observed salesmen and

Lazy Traveler's City Walk

Tram in Calcutta

saleswomen passing by shouting out the goodies they were selling. I could buy vegetables, fresh fish, rice, all kind of snacks, garments, utensils, and the list goes on. They walked the streets all day.

When not sitting on the front porch, my favorite city tour was to ride the number 2B bus from College Street to Ballygaunge. At that time, the 2B bus was a bright red double-decker. I would climb to the upper deck and walk all the way to the front of the bus. The other riders or the conductor did not mind my standing there with my skinny body. Most of the time, I would get a seat. Watching the road passing quickly back under the bus was thrilling. I would get off the bus as soon as I saw Jasodha Bhawan at the Gariahat four-way intersection. Jasodha Bhawan was a massive building occupying about two city blocks at the junction of Gariahat Road and Rash Behari Avenue. The building is still there. On the outside wall of the building, there were billboards of many sizes, shapes, and colors. The large size of this building was fascinating to me. The houses in my hometown were not small huts but were modest in size. Walking on the clean concrete sidewalk was a pleasure compared to walking on usually unpaved roads without sidewalks, as in my hometown. Stores, small and large, occupied the ground level of Jasodha Bhawan. My main attraction was the saree and jewelry store windows decorated with beautiful saree-clad mannequins. I would stand in front of those dazzling windows and gaze for who knew how long.

On my way back by the 2B bus, I would get down somewhere on Chowringhee Road and walk west toward the Metro cinema lobby. Chowringhee Road was a major arterial road connecting Esplanade to Calcutta's south and eastern neighborhoods. One of my favorite spots was a Bata shoe store. A window was full of colorful women's shoes of all different sizes, shapes, and designs. There was one beautiful pair of women's sandals with a price tag of two hundred twenty rupees. That was a lot of money in 1958. I wondered who could spend that much on a pair of shoes. And how beautiful her feet would look with those sandals on.

A visit to Dalhousie Square with Dilip was another adventure for me. Dilip, the son of my aunt's neighbor Mr. Anil Roy, was near my age and my partner in crime. He knew where to go for the cheapest and spiciest street food and how to buy movie tickets for the neighborhood movie theater named Purobi. The movie theaters would not sell tickets to underage children. Dilip knew

Coal-fired small stove

Bishu da, a ticket counter person. He would tell him that he needed two tickets for his elder brother. Bishu da would oblige, no questions asked. The word "da" is a short version of Dada. In Bengali culture, a younger person will show respect and address an older male as Dada. Dilip would bribe Bishu with small changes and other goodies. One time he bribed Bishu with a few cigarettes he stole from his dad's packet.

One morning Dilip told me that he would go to his dad's office and I could go with him. His dad worked in the Writers Building in Dalhousie Square. I asked permission from my aunt. She consented and gave me two rupees for pocket money. By about 9 am on that day, we were out with Mr. Roy. We boarded a tramcar to Dharmatala, one of the larger business districts and a transportation hub of Calcutta. Trams and buses were crisscrossing Dharmatala from all corners of Calcutta. Our tram stopped at Esplanade Tram Depot. We got off and jumped into a Howrah-bound tram that would take us to the Writers Building in Dalhousie Square. Howrah is another town across the river, connected to Calcutta

Writers Building

by a bridge. Mr. Roy worked for the state government in an office in the Writers Building. It was hard for me to control my excitement. I wanted to jump and run on the sidewalk. I could not, as my aunt told me repeatedly to stay with Dilip. Obviously, my aunt knew that I was not a city kid.

The Writers building had two side entrances and one main entrance in the middle, on the Dalhousie Square side. We entered through the east entrance, where the entry control was located. It was not a security check at that time. It was more like crowd control. Employees used their identity cards as their entry permits. A visitor would tell the person sitting at the front desk the name of the official they wished to see. The clerk would check the name and verify it was on the list. Then he would write a ticket with the official's name and the floor number of his office. The visitor will show that paper at the entrance door to gain entry.

There was a long line in front of us. What would all these people do inside? Were they visitors like us? Mr. Roy told me that people from all over West Bengal come to this building. The head offices of the government agencies were inside the Writers Building. The entire scene was fascinating to me. This was a new experience. I had never been inside an office building, let alone an enormous one like the Writers Building. The only office I was familiar with was the one-room, small school office. The Block Development Office was about half a mile from our house. This office was in a one-storied, slightly bigger than a residential house. I never went inside that office. Dilip broke my spell by tapping on my shoulder and passing a ticket to me. We followed Mr. Roy. I was nervous and grasped Dilip's hand.

Another first-time adventure opportunity arose inside – riding in an elevator. Known as a "lift" in India, riding it to the 3rd floor was out of a world experience for me. Exiting the lift, we entered a big room. Inside the room, there were rows of tables. Each table had one or two chairs. Most tables had only one. The tables held stacks of brown file folders. The stacks reached as high as my forehead. Mr. Roy walked to his desk and sat on his chair. A man quickly appeared and mumbled something in Mr. Roy's ear. Then the gentleman pulled two chairs and set them up near Mr. Roy's chair. I learned later from Dilip that the man was a peon. He helped the clerical staff working in that office room. His name was Madhab.

Mr. Roy asked us to sit, and we did. Madhab came back with a tea kettle and disposable cups. He poured tea into a cup and placed it in front of Mr. Roy. Madhab asked if Mr. Roy needed anything else. Mr. Roy looked at Dilip. Dilip said he wanted a toast. Mr. Roy looked at me. I had no idea what to order. I quickly followed Dilip and just said, "A toast." Mr. Roy started working, and we sat there quietly. In a few minutes, Madhab appeared with two plates. It was a day for breaking one new ground after another. In our town, there was no bakery, and thus bread was not an everyday item. We ate handmade flatbreads like tortillas. That piece of bread was thick, cut out of a big loaf and toasted, with a lot of butter on both sides and sprinkled with sugar on both sides. I was taking it slow and savoring my toast. On the other hand, Dilip devoured his toast and urged me to finish. I obliged and gobbled up my bread, and was ready to go. Mr. Roy told us to come back by 1 o'clock for lunch. We planned to have lunch in the cafeteria and go back home.

Dilip knew his way around and was almost running, with me dragging behind. We took the lift, which was empty then, and descended to the street level. We exited via the east side entrance just as we had come in. We crossed two streets and ended up on an open road between office buildings. I saw two poles on the opposite side of the road and a rope hanging between the poles above the road. There were people circled all around, two to three deep. There was almost no vehicular traffic. I noticed two cars pass by under the taut rope. The crowd parted and made a clearing in the middle so that the vehicles could pass.

In the middle of the road, a man dressed in a colorful Kurta, like a magician, played a hand-held drum as he danced around. A little girl and a monkey were also dancing with the drumbeats. The monkey, dressed like a human child, had a small red t-shirt and ankle-length pants. The little girl had a red kurta and white pajamas. The drummer started beating faster and louder. The monkey jumped onto the pole on the street's right side and climbed to the top. The girl followed the monkey and started to climb the pole. When the monkey reached the top, at the drummer's visual and verbal prompts, the monkey jumped on the rope, hung upside down for a few seconds, and scurried to the other end of the rope. The crowd applauded, and the drummer started dancing.

Next, the girl stepped on the rope with a balancing bar in front of her. The drum stopped, and the people around became dead quiet. The girl was taking small steps forward while balancing herself on the rope. She slid down the pole to the ground as soon as she reached the rope's end. The crowd seemed to gasp all at once. Now we heard a deep sigh of relief. She and the monkey took a few victory laps while the drummer frantically beat his drum. The

monkey picked up a basket with a few coins and rupee bills lying in the bottom. The monkey and the girl began walking around, asking for bakshis (tips).

I was enjoying the scene, especially the monkey snatching bills and coins from the hands of the viewers. Dilip pulled my arm and started walking to the next adventure. I asked where we were heading. He said, "To the GPO." GPO was the abbreviation of General Post Office. I was wondering what attraction was there - buying a postcard? No way – Dilip told me there was a vendor that sells bhutta (corn on the cob) for twenty-five paise. A paise was one-hundredth of a rupee. On the east side of the GPO, there was the bhuttawala. An Indian bhutta was like sweet corn on the cob. Bhuttawala was a person who sold bhutta. He had a small charcoal stove in front of him. There was corn on the cob on a metal grate on the fire. We ordered two bhuttas with salt and hot pepper. He picked two charred cobs, pressed pieces of lime on the hot corn on the cob, and sprinkled salt and pepper.

Munching our corns, we walked around Dalhousie Square. Dilip led us to the east of the pond, Lal Dighi, on the Old Court House Steet. I was looking around while walking, just like a wide-eyed country boy, struggling to absorb the many eye-catching events around us. Dilip pulled my arm as a signal to stop and look on the side of the street. A family of three – a mother and two children, sleeping on the concrete sidewalk. At first, I did not observe anything special. Then I saw a small aluminum bowl, on the sidewalk, with a few coins in it. The mother and the children were not moving at all. They looked lifeless. We saw one passerby drop coins in the bowl. It was amazing how even the children remained motionless for as long as we were there. I did not see any of them even blink. Dilip said he saw the family often during his visits to his dad's office. He never saw them awake.

Just before lunchtime, we returned to the east entrance of the Writers Building and joined

Above   Kolkata Gari Baranda

Right   Bus pushing water over a car

the line for the piece of paper. I was watching Dilip. He wrote his name, my name, and his dad's name on specific columns. The clerk gave him a piece of paper, and we were on our way. We met Mr. Roy in the cafeteria. The cafeteria was a large room with many open booths. Most of the booths had four chairs around a square table. Mr. Roy ordered a full Bengali lunch, complete with rice, fish curry, and dal. I was waiting and watching Dilip. He ordered goat liver curry. I had no idea what to order, so I followed Dilip's footsteps and ordered liver curry. The first few spoonsful of liver curry were not too tasty. It had a sort of earthy flavor. However, it was cheap, it was spicy, and the portion was generous. I visited Writers Building at lunchtime, often in my youth and early adult life, just to have a goat liver curry lunch. All I had to do was remember the name of anybody working in the building to get the piece of paper and get in.

I realized the Writers Building and the GPO were quite different from the other buildings in the neighborhood. Most other buildings were utilitarian with straight-line designs. That does not mean that the functional design of buildings was inferior. In fact, it was the opposite. The modern designs made the building stronger, more practical, and cheaper to build. The Writers Building and the GPO were not very practical by today's standards. Still, they are beautiful buildings with a treasure trove of history.

The British East India Company constructed the present-day Writers Building. This building was one of the first three-storied buildings in

Calcutta. The architectural design of the building was Gothic style, also referred to as Victorian Style. British and French architects brought Victorian styles into the Calcutta buildings in the seventeenth century. This gigantic building is also known, in Bengali, as the Mahakaran. The original Writers Building was smaller and simpler in design. That small building was a residence for the East India Company's junior writers. Thus, the name Writers Building stuck to this new building forever. The West Bengal government used this building as its Secretariat. The Writers Building name changed to the Bengali name Mahakaran at that time. For many years, the office of the West Bengal Chief Minister was in this building.

The GPO building had completed in 1864. The building is still in use and serves as the central post office of Calcutta and a major post office of West Bengal. The signature aspects of the building are the 228-foot-high dome, the Corinthian columns, and a huge clock at the base of the dome. As with the Writers Building, the GPO carries the Greco-Roman architectural design imported by the British East Indian Company.

The Lal Dighi (red pond) is in the middle of Dalhousie Square. The Bengali word Dighi refers to an artificial pond. The Bengali word Lal means red. Historic buildings like the Writers Building, GPO, Andrews Church, and High Court are around Lal Dighi.

When I was attending college, I used Calcutta as a place to change trains to go home. I would get off a train at Howrah

Left Men and boys pushing a car
Right Esplanade Tram Depot to Writer's Building

station, take a bus ride to Sealdah station and take another train home. During that time, Calcutta used to slide away in front of my eyes like movie scenes. West Bengal, especially Calcutta, experienced a turbulent time in the seventies. There was a battle for the political and social soul of the people of Bengal. Political violence was happening throughout West Bengal and especially in Calcutta every day. This violence was an essential part of the popularly known Naxalite Movement. The movement started in 1967; the most violent phase was over by 1973. Over the course of those few years, Calcutta changed. The shopkeepers took over the sidewalks and streets. In some places, mountains of garbage blocked the road and sidewalks. Everything in Calcutta seemed to have increased enormously. That included population, cars, buses, push carts, bikes, and trash.

I survived the turmoil of the seventies and discovered myself with a romantic connection in Calcutta. It was there that I met my wife for the first time. She was born and raised in Calcutta; we were married and honeymooned in the city. Time passed like water under the Howrah Bridge, or, should I say, into the Atlantic Ocean. At the same time, I was busy working, raising a family, and running errands in Albany, New York.

In 1995 the city of Paris reminded me of Calcutta. That summer, I was visiting Paris with my wife and son. We were walking to the Louvre Museum from Pyramid Metro station on the concrete sidewalk of Rue De

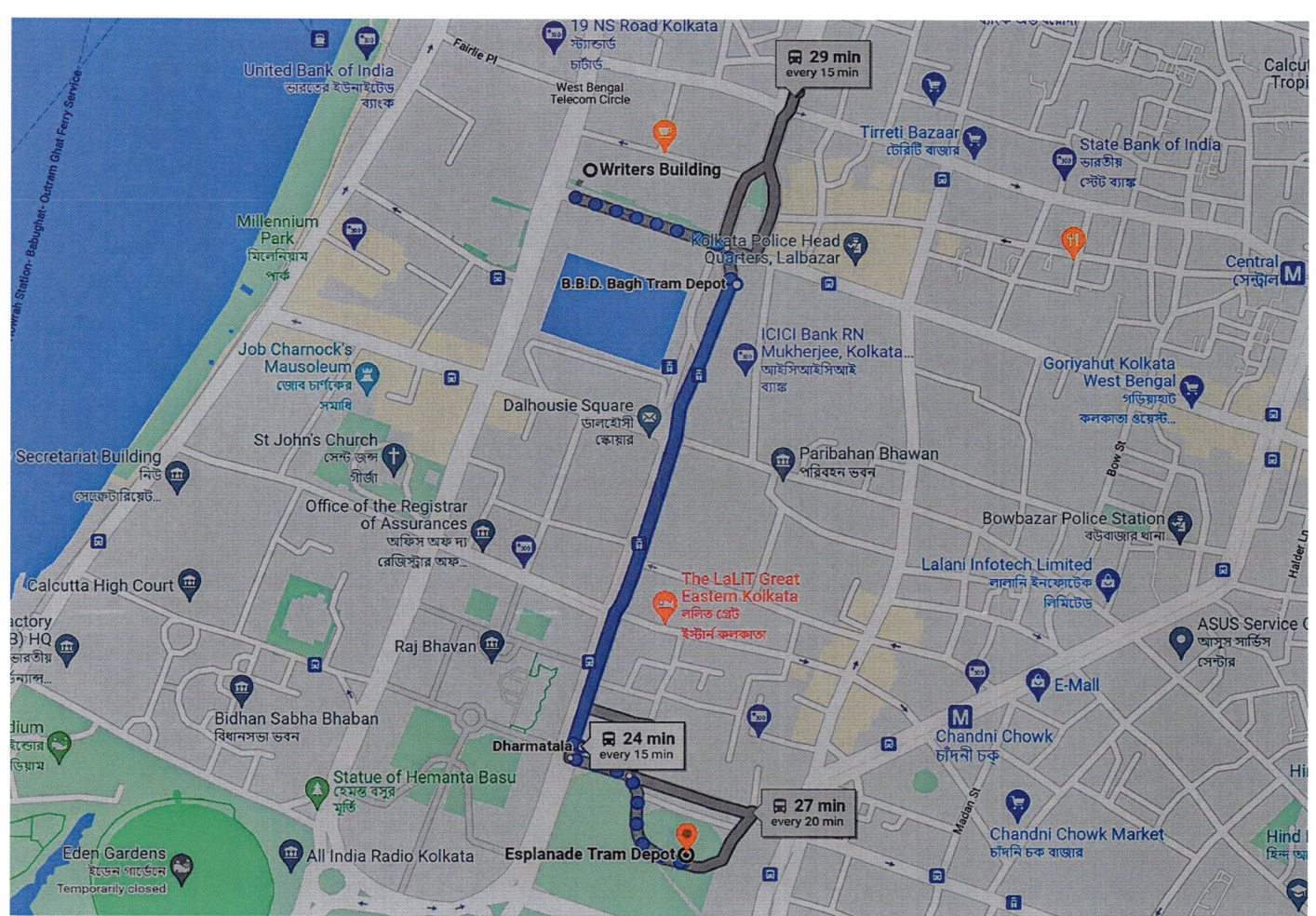

Rivoli. However, it could have been Red Road or Dalhousie Square of Calcutta. The clean wide road and sidewalk, the stone buildings' foundation walls rising at the end of the sidewalk, and the Greco-Roman architecture of the buildings all looked familiar. One morning, I saw city workers in blue uniforms cleaning Paris Street, just below our hotel window, with brooms and water hoses. Like in Calcutta, the city workers would clean the roads not too long ago. A musty smell came out of the stone foundation of the building we had just passed. This was the same smell I had while walking around the buildings in Dalhousie Square. The sights and smell transported me back to Calcutta, near the General Post Office building. Even the panhandlers were similar. I remembered the women with one or two children in ragged clothing lying on the sidewalk in Dalhousie Square. I saw a similar scene in Paris on Rue De Rivoli. There was a woman with three children on the sidewalk. It looked like they were in a deep sleep.

We traveled to Calcutta from Paris. It was the first week of September. The last few days, it rained heavily in Calcutta; rain was pouring the entire night. I was surprised by the general calm in the morning. The usual honking of the cars and bus roaring was not there. I looked down, and I knew the reason. I could not see the road. It looked like a small river flowing around the houses. The water level was almost as high as the ground-floor entrance.

Calcutta had changed and continued to change at a rapid pace. I felt like Rip Van Winkle. Over the last twenty years, I passed by Calcutta, conducted official business there, took trains, flew in and out by airplane, shopped, and visited friends and family. I missed the changes that went around in the city. The garbage dumps on the sidewalk and roadbeds were gone, the traffic lights were working, and most cars stopped at red lights. My travel to Europe jolted me to look around the mystery city of my childhood. There was an avalanche of name changes. Mirzapur Street was renamed Surya Sen Street, Harrison Road to Mahatma Gandhi Road, Dalhousie Square to Binoy Badal Dinesh Bagh, DumDum Airport to Netaji Subhas Chandra Bose International Airport, and so many others! My childhood's favorite rides, the double-decker bus and trams, were almost extinct. Calcutta State Transportation Corporation started to reduce the number of double-decker buses in the nineties. The last bus was taken out of service in 2005. The reason was that these buses were too expensive to run. The trams were considered too slow for modern traffic, and tramlines occupied too much space. Only a few tram routes were still operating.

Commercial and residential building construction was going on all over the city. The flyovers (long, wide roads over another road) seemed to pop up at the major intersections. I took a Metro train from Kalighat station to Park Street. The metro system was one of the cleanest and cheapest I have experienced. And talk about the culture change, especially youth culture. I had never heard of Mother's Day, Father's Day, or Valentine's Day celebrations in Calcutta until my 1995 visit. These American-style celebrations brought mixed feelings, although, at that time, they were not too widespread. However, they were part of a series of subtle signs that significant cultural changes were in the making.

On that morning, there was almost no traffic except the

Right above   Calcutta, west Bengal, India (Being Map).

Right below Triangle Metro to Louver, Parise, France (Being Map).

Calcutta becomes Kolkata

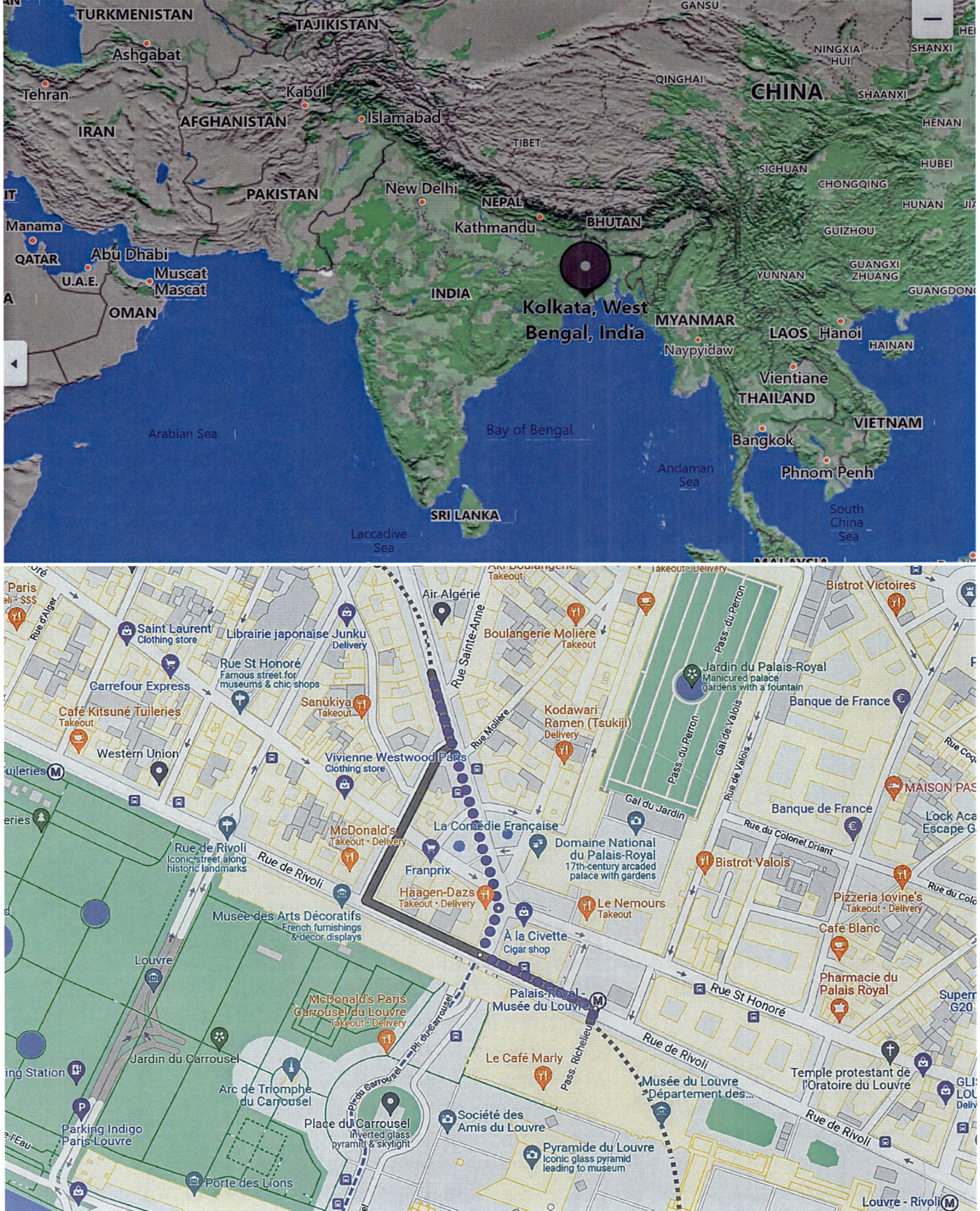

14

Dalhousie Square (google map)

occasional rickshaw puller, on the road below, in front of the building. A fruit and vegetable vendor pushed his cart into the knee-deep water near the milk depot. The milk depot was the small shed on the side of the road. Every morning a milk van dropped off bottles for distribution. People had milk cards to buy bottles at a subsidized price from the depot. I wanted to get some fruits from the vendor and talk to him about the storm. I asked when the water would be gone. He thought it would take about two days and pointed his finger to the concrete pipes stacked on the side of the road. Only the top few inches of the pipes above the floodwater were visible. The city would lay the pipes under the street to pump out the water. That construction was a little late for this storm. I went up to the porch, returned to my chair, and began to munch on a delicious apple.

Soon, I heard the ting-a-ling of a hand-pulled rickshaw and looked down, and I saw the rickshaw and a small car. The car was slowly moving on the street below. It looked like it was floating more than half submerged under muddy water. Right at that time, a bus came along, making huge waves. A wave reached almost up to the rooftop of the car. The bus was gone, but the car stayed there. The engine died, and it would not start. A few adults and little boys, ten to twelve years old, gathered around the car in minutes. Two adults and two boys started to push the car. I was thinking, "Who is the owner of this car, and how could he let the little boys push his car? And how about the parents of those boys? Did not they know that their boys did not even have enough clothes and they may get sick or hurt? Why were they on the street in the muddy water at this time of the morning?" Then I realized it was Calcutta.

The city has survived for over three hundred years. Calcutta was moving forward. Soon the boys would push the car out of the water. Soon there would be morning and sunshine. Soon the water would be gone; the honking of the cars and roar of the buses would be back. The soft light of an autumn morning would shine on the big banner over the milk depot, announcing Sarbojanin Durgoutsabha. The banner announced the upcoming annual Durga Pooja festival. In no time, the whole city would explode into shopping and celebration. Will Calcutta be like Paris again? Calcutta became Kolkata in the year 2001.

Barcelona - The Street Lamp

I woke up from my catnap. Our tour bus suddenly stopped with a jolt. It was not like an earthquake. However, it was strong enough to shake the sleepy heads. The bus stopped at a traffic light. It had been traveling at highway speed for over an hour. The stop broke the rhythm. This meant that the bus had entered Barcelona. Our bus was a typical modern-day industrial-size tour bus. And Barcelona was a modern-day city

left Barcelona Streetlamp

Top Kolkata Gaslight

with a long trail of history. I looked out of the bus window. We were on a six-lane, divided city street in a diverse neighborhood. High-rise and mid-rise buildings lined up on both sides of the street. Retail stores, restaurants, and cafes occupied the ground levels of the buildings, as often occurs in similar cities. We were traveling from Salou, a seaside resort town in Spain. It took us about an hour and a half to arrive in Barcelona.

This was my first time in Spain, and Salou was the first city I entered. A Thomas Cook flight from New Castle, England, brought us to Reus Airport. Reus was about eight miles and twenty minutes bus ride to Salou Inter2 Aparthotel. The hotel had apartments of various sizes with housekeeping facilities. It was like a resort, with dining facilities, a bar, a swimming pool, and evening entertainment. The hotel was a few minutes from the beach. The restaurant was in a brightly lit large dining hall on the lower level. For food lovers, the vast European-style buffet breakfast could be a destination by itself. The countless food selections included desserts and non-alcoholic drinks in that buffet.

Lazy Traveler's City Walk

Salou Inter2 Aparthotel Apartment Resort

Saluo Lazy Hazy Afternoon

There was no way anybody would go away hungry from that food heaven. Inter2 hosted participatory entertainment sessions every evening. The resort singer would set up a stage with an audio system and start playing their instruments and singing popular songs. The residents would begin walking in as singles or groups and sit around on the sofas in the lounge. The lead singer would invite the audience to participate. In no time, the floor would be packed with moving, gyrating, and dancing men, women, and children.

This trip to Salou was also my first experience with the Mediterranean culture, especially Spanish culture and lifestyle. In my mind, siesta was strongly associated with the Spanish lifestyle. In the 1990s, technology, financial, and trade globalization were spreading. There were stories in the news media about North American companies struggling to adjust to the lifestyle and culture of other countries like Spain. Siesta, the long afternoon break, was one of the practices some American companies struggled to manage. The word 'siesta' brought a pleasing, relaxing, and dreamy afternoon feeling to mind. The word meant an afternoon nap on a hot-weather day. It was particularly attractive after a heavy satisfactory mid-day meal. A version of siesta was prevalent in many parts of the world, including the Mediterranean and India. The afternoons, in the warm weather regions, get uncomfortably hot. The evenings, on the other hand, are relatively cooler and more comfortable. The siesta provided welcome relief. In modern days with energy-efficient air-conditioned office buildings, siesta has lost favor.

In 2001, India officially renamed the city of Calcutta to Kolkata. In and around areas of the then Calcutta, there was a time when most of the retail stores and some other businesses closed for the afternoon hours. Between mid-day and about 4

Saluo Cafe di Mare Cocktail

Casa Milà

o'clock in the afternoon, the retail areas used to be lonely and quiet, with low vehicular and foot traffic. As time progressed and globalization took over, the tradition of siesta has all but crept out from most urban areas of India and other parts of the world.

When we visited Salou, Spain, in 2011, I thought there would be a strong presence of the siesta tradition. On our second day in Salou, we considered a day trip to Barcelona. Being so close, a one-and-a-half-hour bus ride to Barcelona, visiting was a must. All the partners in crime agreed and said, yea. On that day, after lunch, we left our hotel to search for a travel agent to buy a Barcelona travel package for the next day. This was the first afternoon we were outside in the shopping area. On the first full day in Salou, in the afternoon, we were on the beach and then in our room taking - what else? Siesta!

On that day, we observed that the shopping areas, which consisted of every street around the hotel, including the boardwalk, were quieter and low in foot and vehicular traffic. The city buses were nowhere to be seen. These buses go around the shopping district every few minutes. Most of the stores and retail services were open but with few shoppers. Some service establishments like travel agents had their doors wide open without anybody minding the store. We walked into a store, through the wide-open storefront, and browsed around, hoping that somebody would show up from the back of the store to help us. When we realized that nobody was minding the store, we were a little perplexed and went out searching for the next open place. This time we looked for at least one human figure inside the store before stepping in. After walking for a while, we were in front of a place with a human figure stationed behind a desk. There were travel posters and brochures on the walls. We bought our tickets for a guided bus tour leaving for Barcelona the next day at 8:30 in the morning. I asked the agent what was happening with the stores – there was nobody to help us. He said, "Oh, it is the siesta time; they will return at four." We believed him. We decided to respect the local tradition and be part of the community. We quickly went back to our hotel and indulged in blissful siestas.

In the next few days, I talked with the hotel front desk staff and store clerks in the shopping district about the siesta. I realized the siesta was no longer as dreamy and blissful as I thought. Most people take a short afternoon break. Usually, no siesta comes along – the breaks were filled with running errands and a quick lunch. The retail stores and restaurants adjusted their working hours to European Union standards. In the resort areas, there were not too many souvenir hunters in the afternoons on weekdays in the semi-tourist season of June. In the mid-day, the retail business community keeps stores closed or staffing levels low. After the siesta, we woke up refreshed and full of energy. We charged out for another shopping spree on that particular day.

The shopping areas around the hotel and along the beach were transformed back to their usual – should I say business! The streets were packed with traffic flow, and sidewalks were full of men, women, and little people. The little people were on baby carriages, dad's shoulders, mom's arms, and their own little feet. And they were jumping, running, screaming, and licking ice cream. Everybody was dressed, looking

Casa Batlló

Casa Amatller

fresh, and ready to enjoy another spring evening.

The shops were brightly lit and fully staffed and doing brisk business. The traffic cops showed up at the intersections, and the local buses were making trips every few minutes. Like elsewhere in the retail world, especially in Spain, the evenings were the time to do business and make money. In Spain, the evening extends into late night with a siesta or without. The bars and restaurants played music and were full of patrons. And why would they not be full!

Cafe di Mare was on the beach and was right in front of us. The cafe was serving the most elaborately garnished cocktails I have ever seen in my life. We were like sleepwalkers, following the large clientele, and almost were sucked into the bar. We ordered the exotic-looking cocktails and started to sip. It felt like forever. The evening crept into the late night—by the time we left the bar, it was well past midnight.

Our guide Angela's loud announcement brought me back to Barcelona. She told us to look outside the bus. The bus was on Passeig de Gracia, Barcelona's most famous street and probably the most expensive street for real estate. It was a six-lane city street with mid to high-rise commercial and residential buildings on both sides. This street had Barcelona's most famous buildings, hotels, and designer brand outlets. Our guide drew our attention to the building designed by Antonio Gaudi – the Casa Mila, also known as the la Pedrera. We had a few minutes to watch the roadside beauty. The bus started to roll and picked up city speed and took, I think, a right turn. Our guide alerted us to look at two more of Barcelona's famous buildings – Casa Batllo and Casa

Barcelona streetlamp fire box

Placa de Catalunya, the famous town square. That was the first two hour-stop in Barcelona. It seemed there was another stop before reaching the town square.

The bus slowed and stopped close to the curb. Her Highness, our guide, Angel's voice came over the audio, and she ordered us to look at a street lamp to our left. She mentioned that this was a bonus stop and would be a quick one. The lamp was outside my window, across the opposite traffic lanes. It was a type of lamppost I had never seen before. This unusual street lamp had an ornate metal post, with a matched decorative lamp at the top hanging from the post. The post's bottom had a bench in the back and two doors in the front. The front looked like a firebox. The bench and the firebox were constructed with broken tiles mosaic. There were thirty-two of these lamps on this famous street. These lamps were designed in 1906 by Pere Falques, a Modernist architect.

I listened to the story coming out of the audio system and watched the lamps. The bus started to move, and I had just enough time to take a few photos. I was thinking about the two doors in front of the base of the lamps. The bus crawled past the set of traffic lights and turned right. We were close to

Amatller on the right side of the bus. An architect professor of Antonio Gaudi built the Casa Batllo. Antonio Gaudi was the most famous architect of Spain from 1852 to 1926. The building we just saw was destined to be demolished to make room for another project. Antonio Gaudi saved Casa Batllo in 1904, changed the inside and the facade, and thus converted it into a work of art. Just next to Casa Batllo was Casa Amaatller. Josep Puig I Cadafalch, another famous architect of the same era, designed this building. I took a few photos while I was listening to the audio.

I checked the company brochure for site seeing stops. Our next stop would have been

Barcelona streetlamp stone seats

our first official stop of the day – Placa de Catalunya. It is the main square of the city and the largest in Spain. Our guide started her instruction and alerts sounding like a flight attendant delivering flight safety instructions. One of the alerts was commonplace in most cities I visited in the Eurozone. That was about the pickpockets. She warned us that the thieves had descended with new skills for the new tourist season. She said if we were not paying attention, the thieves were so skilled that they could untie our shoes and go away with them; we would not even know or feel a thing.

Our bus stopped in the Placa de Catalunya in a designated parking area. A few other fat belly tour buses lined up in front of us. At the end of the two-hour excursion, we would return to that spot to catch our bus and continue our tour. I considered asking Angela a few questions about the Pere Falques lamps. As usual, I was slow to disembark and observed a group of fellow travelers already surrounding her. By the time I could go close to her, she was scurrying off to her own lunch adventure. I was desperate and stopped her. I asked her about the box at the bottom of the lamppost. She was not too happy about the interruption. However, she was professional and maintained a smile. She then told the story. In the old days, the city lit charcoal fires in those boxes in the winter evenings. The Barcelonans, after the siesta, used to come out for shopping, eating out, and socializing. They could warm up in the cold winter evenings, sitting on the warm stone benches or mill around the street lamps with the fireboxes.

As we observed in Salou, the evenings were and still are important in Spain for social and business reasons. It was natural for the business community and the city to make the evening crowd comfortable. Hence, they stay longer, stay out

Baecelona Plaça de Catalunya Pigeons

of their homes, and spend money in stores. The city's hotels, restaurants, and entertainment outfits were willing to indulge the clients. It was like a deep-state conspiracy to keep the Barcelonans in the shopping and entertainment district as long and late as possible. Our guide started walking away before I could ask another question. Now she answered one question but raised ninety-nine other unanswered.

I think the vertical structure of the lamps was constructed with wrought iron. The use of steel started later in 1900. The hanging globe at the top of the post looked like an electric fixture. It could be a retrofitted modern-day electric bulb. General Electric patented the tungsten filament bulb in 1906, and mass production started in 1910. The lampposts were constructed in 1906. These lamps probably did not have tungsten filament electric bulbs. Electric arc lamps were in use around that time. These lamps might have been fitted with electric arc-type bulbs. If not electric, they would have been gas-fired. Then all kinds of mundane logistical questions arise – how were the gas lamps lighted in the evening and turned off in the morning? In Calcutta, in the late 1950s, there were a few remaining gas street lamps on some forgotten streets. As a pre-teen boy, I remember seeing a lamplighter with a ladder on his shoulder walking along. He climbed up every morning to turn off the gas

Lazy Traveler's City Walk

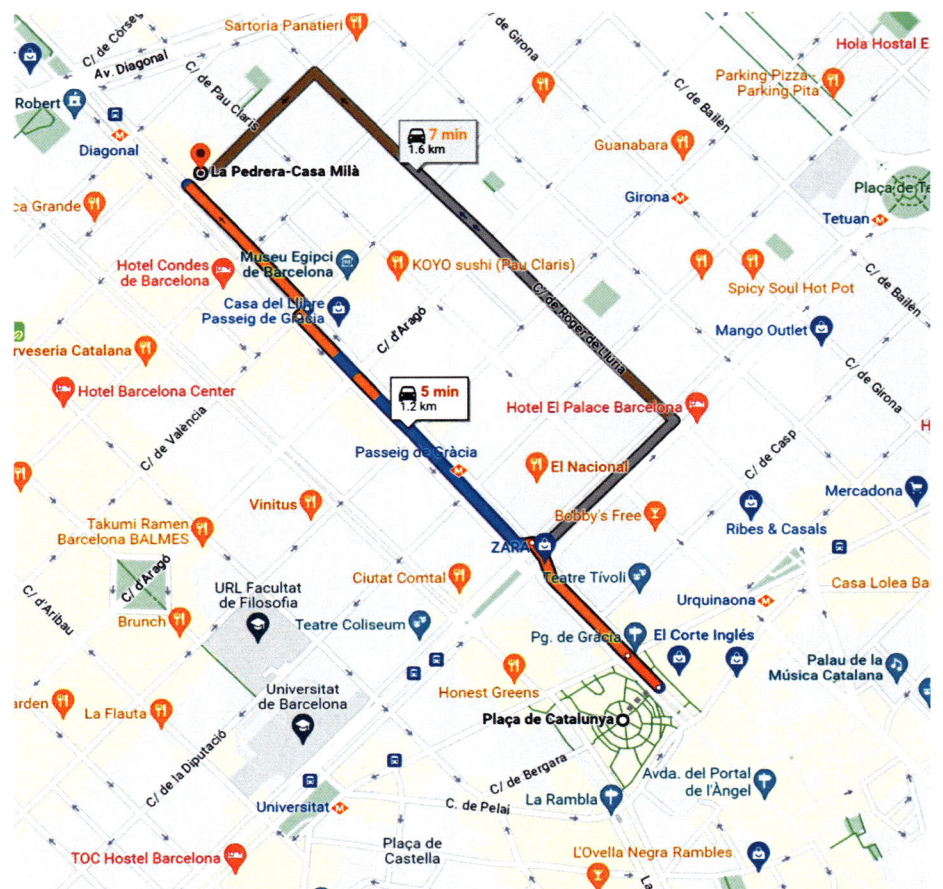

Top Barcelona Streetlamp - photo taken through the bus window.

Left Casa Mila to Plaça de Catalunya

Below Salou to Barcelona

lamp in front of the house I was staying. He would come back every evening to turn it on.

The Passeig de Gracia lamps are too tall to climb up and down daily to turn them off in the morning and on in the evening if they were gas lamps. Were the lamps kept on all the time? These lamps were part of the lifestyle and culture of the Barcelonans in the recent past. The story of these lamps connects the lifestyle of lazy, hazy days with dreamy siestas.

So why did the bus not have a longer stop at the lamp? The lamp stop was a bonus. It turned out to be the most exciting stop for me. The focus of that tour was the famous and popular attractions. The lamp did not get elevated to that level. I had no knowledge of these lamps before I saw them that day through the bus window. Thanks to Angela for making that surprise stop. If I were a hotshot researcher, I would have checked into a hotel and dived into in-depth research. On the other hand, the lazy traveler in me dreamed of a slow and lazy tour of the city sometime in the future.

Our guide Angela alerted us about the pickpockets. However, she forgot to tell us about the hundreds of pigeons in the square. The pigeons flocked around us as soon as we stepped into the square. Some of the pigeons started to peck on our shoes. I thought they had been poorly trained by the pickpockets. The pigeons needed more training to loosen the laces and steal our shoes. Feeding and watching the pigeons could be a stop by itself. Lunchtime was fast approaching, and we would have to catch our bus soon. We spotted Valentino's Tapas - Bar- Restaurant on the other side of the square. That was our lunch destination - no marching orders needed. We were already marching to Valentino's.

On that day in Barcelona, though, I saw no sign of siestas. The square was crowded with office workers, retail shoppers, lunch eaters, visitors, and pigeons. Lots of pigeons.

Juliet of Verona

Our industrial-size tour bus stopped just across from the Arena Di Verona. Most tourists call it Verona Arena. It was a Roman Amphitheater built in the first century. Our destination for the day was the city of Verona in Italy. We would visit Casa Di Giulietta. Tourist friends called it – Juliet's House. It was not the first visit for a group of fellow travelers. At that time, I was not sure what brought them back. Later I learned that these visits were like a pilgrimage for my traveler

Left   Juliet's Balcony

Above Juliet's Bronze Statue

friends.

We took a giant leap from New York J. F. Kennedy Airport over the Atlantic. We landed at Leonardo da Vinci airport in Rome. We stayed for three days in Rome at the Albany Hotel. On the fourth day, at 8 AM, our bus was at the hotel parking lot, ready to take us across the country. Our bus was scheduled to stop at Assisi, Florence, Padua, Venice, Verona, and finally, Milan. The Adige River flows across Verona. The city is in the Veneto region of Italy. We ended our trip in Milan and flew back home from Milan Malpensa Airport.

Arriving in Verona, our bus stopped. I saw our tour director, Jennifer, get off the bus and position herself strategically with her flag, which looked like a small folded umbrella, in her left hand. She did not quite raise the umbrella yet. Before getting off the bus, our director went over her usual health and safety alerts. They were the exact instructions she gave us at every other city stop. She advised us to be alert and careful about our valuables in crowded locations. The purse snatchers and pickpockets have arrived along with the tourists. The miscreants were aggressive and

Piazza Bra, The main square of Verona. This is the largest square in Europe.

armed with new skills and techniques. The purse snatchers quietly moved around the tables in the outdoor cafes. They were looking for unattended items or items right in front of the unmindful, red-wine-drinking, souvenir-hunting, easygoing, relaxing tourists.

In front of the bus, our fellow travelers started to disembark and line up behind our fearless director. I got up, wedged myself between my seat and the back of the seat in front of me, and stretched myself up to the luggage rack. I was getting my provisions for the day from the big bag. The provisions, including a small bottle of water, would go into a small carry bag.

I did not see a single public drinking water fountain throughout my entire time in Italy. In Rome, there were fountains everywhere. Water spraying out of them, flowing out of them, seeping out of them, and spewing out of them all over Rome. Suppose you are looking for a drinking water fountain – good luck. A bottle of water and a glass of wine cost almost the same. In my carry bag, a small water bottle used to be reassuring. Then there were the few pieces of granola bars for snacking to be taken along. By the time I got my stuff, the bus was almost empty. Our driver, a very polite man, was patiently waiting near the exit steps for us. He got used to my lackluster disembarkation routine. Hey – I am going for a site seeing tour, not to testify before Congress. Is that a good analogy? A congressional testimony sure sounds serious, and no witness dares be late for a deposition.

When the bus stopped at Verona, I saw the Arena on my left when I looked through the bus window. It is the fourth largest of all the Roman arenas in Italy and one of the best-preserved structures of its kind.

Verona Palazzo del Commune, This Neoclassical style 1848 building serves as Verona City Hall

On our right were the remnants of a Roman-era high wall. I remember seeing these high walls, or whatever remained of them, in most cities we visited in Italy. The wall reminded me of an old prison in India, protected by high granite walls along the perimeter. We, the bus full of travelers, got off the bus and formed a line right along the wall behind our tour director. We were like a chain gang slogging behind our prison guard, ready to march forward along the road just outside a prison. Our guard raised her flag right at that moment, and the march started.

We walked into the Arena end of Piazza Bra, Verona's main town square. We were in front of the Palazzo Barbieri, the Verona City Hall. The restaurants were on the opposite side of the Piazza. The famous palaces and ancient buildings were around its perimeter. We did not have much time to spend in the Piazza and would proceed to our main attraction for the day—Juliet's House.

We gathered around our director in front of the City Hall. She told us how to get to Juliet's House. The directions were not complicated, and it was not far - about a ten-minute walk. We would return to the City Hall by 12:30 PM to catch our bus. We started walking on Via Giuseppe Mazzini from the City Hall with those instructions under our belts. In about ten minutes, we took a right turn on Via Cappello. The address of Juliet's House was Via Cappello, 23, 37121 Verona VR, Italy.

If we had to navigate to that address all by ourselves, it might not have been just ten minutes. The road signs were in Italian – remember? My helpful friends back home and many online experts advised me to learn Italian before traveling. I did not

Arena di Verona, one of the best-kept Roman era arenas, it is still used for events with large audience.

wish to disappoint my friends and well-wishers. I decided to learn basic Italian and did what any modern-day man would have done. I ordered a few books and CDs from Amazon and had them delivered the next day.

I got busy before the travel. Resolving issues regarding my passport, visa, foreign exchange, hotel reservation, travel insurance, health insurance, lawn mowing during my absence, and the main event of packing the suitcases was overwhelming. And especially the packing. I gathered my stuff in a few piles and started to dump them inside the suitcase. I put the Amazon packet first so that I would not forget it. They were buried under the clothes and other sixty-five different odd items in the suitcase. I made sure that I would not leave them at home. Good idea, right? The next time I saw the Amazon packet was when I returned home and emptied my suitcase for safe storage in the basement.

You ask, "What happened to your million-dollar phone GPS?" The phone GPS? Well, do not get me started. The SIM card I bought for my phone was not working. Yes – I called the customer service number. The Italian operator was probably very helpful, but I would not

Via Giuseppe Mazzini din Verona, a narrow pedestrian road considered the commercial center of Verona.

know. The only word I understood was "Buongiorno." That was the word our director Jennifer greeted us with every morning as the bus started and she started her morning updates.

As we started walking, we found an easier way to navigate. All we had to do was follow the crowd. People like us were moving towards the same destination. The Via Mazzini was paved with white and reddish Italian marble, and the sides were lined with brightly lit stores of brand-name fashion retailers. The usual cast of characters of high-end brands Prada, Dolce & Gabbana, and Gucci were lined up on both sides of the road. Mixed in with the brand name stores were many affordable local retailers. It was a popular shopping area for tourists as well as the locals. And for a lazy traveler like me – this was an amazing city walk.

Juliet's house was on our left. It was a brick building built in the 13th century. The entrance was a huge gate with an arch at the top. We stepped onto a cobble-stoned courtyard. Juliet's house and balcony were on the right side of the courtyard. A bronze statue of Juliet was on the left, under the balcony, in front of us. On the right side of

Juliet's statue, I saw a gate covered with hundreds of padlocks on the grills. As a tradition, people wrote their names and their lovers' names on the locks. They placed the locks on the gate. They tossed the keys —hoping their hearts would be eternally locked with the hearts of their lovers.

According to the legend, Romeo proposed to Juliet on this balcony in William Shakespeare's play Romeo and Juliet. In the play, this was the balcony where Juliet expressed her love for Romeo for the first time. People get hypnotized thinking about the romantic scene and dialog in the moonlight, as written by Shakespeare. However, the balcony was fake. The play was fiction. The play Romeo and Juliet is set in the city of Verona. Juliet Capulet, obviously, was a fictional character created by William Shakespeare. It is not known if the Bard of Avon ever visited Verona. The only non-fiction reality was the city of Verona. The city created this tourist attraction in the early 20th century.

The Cappello family of Verona owned the house; thus, the imaginary connection to the Capulets Family of William Shakespeare's play was set up. The Montagues and the Capulets families were powerful aristocratic families of Verona. In the twentieth century, the city of Verona purchased the house from the Cappello family to open a museum. Later the city attached a balcony, which it had retrieved from a construction site. The house became famous as Juliet's family home in a few decades. Thus, the legend machine started to

Top Juliet's House Courtyard

Right Love seekers of all ages and from all places

Juliet of Verona

36

Lazy Traveler's City Walk

Left Door full of love locks, locking the hearts of the young lovers forever

Right Juliet's Bronze statue

spin at full speed. Juliet's house has become a tourist attraction.

I saw a most interesting and unexpected sight as I entered the cobbled stone-covered courtyard in Juliet's House. Juliet's bronze statue was surrounded by all kinds of people – men, women, boys, girls, young adults, and senior citizens. The crowd included people of many colors and from many countries. Some of them had already climbed up on the statue's pedestal to touch the statue. They were especially aiming at Juliet's right breast. This interesting behavior was due to another local legend established in modern times. People believe that if they take the time to rub the right breast of the bronze statue, their dream of eternal love will come true.

The city of Verona successfully transformed the Cappello house almost into a shrine. Even though Juliet was a fictional character created by Shakespeare, millions of people started to worship her as a love goddess. Juliet's house has been a place of pilgrimage for traveling people from all over the world.

We came out of Juliet's house's huge stone and brick

Juliet's house - huge stone and brick gate

gate and turned right to go back to the City Hall. We decided to have a cup of coffee before we went back. We went into Venchi Café and settled down with coffee and pastry. While we were having coffee, clouds covered the sky. After coffee, we got out and started backtracking to the City Hall. Light rain has been falling off and on since morning.

As soon as we left the café, the rain started again. The rain started light and quickly turned into pouring rain. I somehow became separated from my fellow travelers. The street in front became a river of umbrella-holding and raincoat-clad figures. The only difference from an actual river was that the river in front of me had umbrellas flowing in both directions simultaneously. The sunlight was gone, and it looked like an evening at noontime. I tried to find my teammates without success. I was not sure which way to go back to the City Hall. I went back to Venchi café to ask for directions. The barista there spoke English. I got directions and decided to wait for the rain to ease up.

Two American tourist families with children were waiting for the rain to stop. I could not control my temptation to have a conversation with them. Conversation with strangers does not come naturally to me. I collected enough courage and dived into one anyway. I asked the woman next to me where she was from. She was from Los Angeles. Her gesture and tone encouraged me

Venchi café

to continue the conversation. I told her that I was from Alexandria, Virginia.

After a few more exchanges of short pleasantries, I asked how she liked Juliet's House. Immediately I noticed a change in her demeanor. I thought she got a little tense. She looked at me and was silent for a moment. Then she said that she was not impressed with the lovey-dovey story of Casa Di Giulietta. She thought the city of Verona was exploiting the image of the girl and the story for the tourist dollar. Why did the city not have a statue of Romeo?

Moreover, Juliet was only thirteen years old in Shakespeare's story. The lady was uncomfortable when her seven-year-old son asked why people touched Juliet's breast. The rain stopped, and she waved goodbye and walked away with her group.

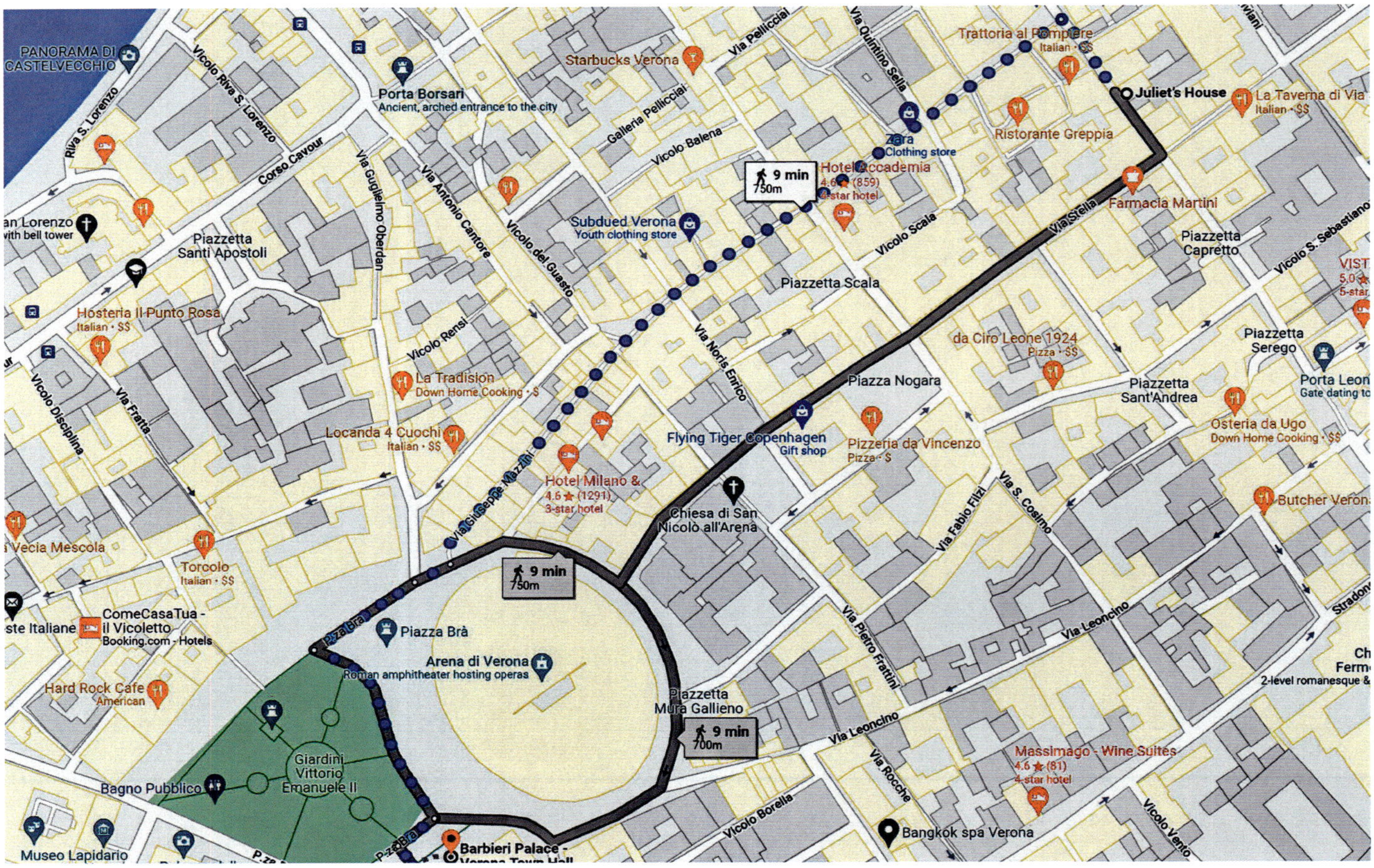

Lazy Traveler's City Walk

Cityhall to Juliet's House

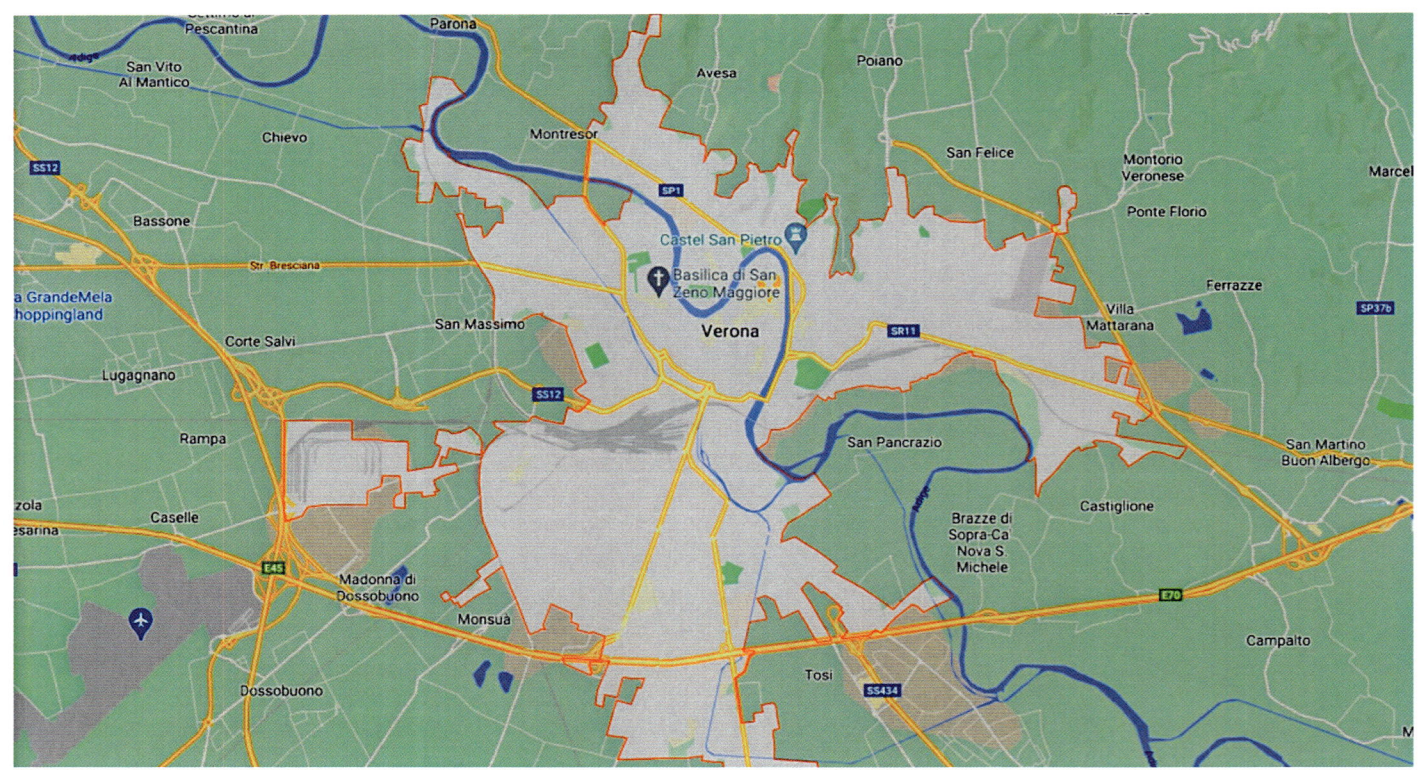

Verona, Italy

Torture at the Tower

Four sisters and three brothers-in-law had descended in London, England. Three sets of Sisters-in-law and brothers-in-law flew in from Boston, Washington DC, and Orlando, Florida. One sister, the only one that was a Royal Subject of Her Majesty the Queen Elizabeth of the United Kingdom, arrived by train. She lives in Whitley Bay, a city near Newcastle upon Tyne in Northern England. The week-long party started on September 3, 2016, in President Hotel. On

Left Queen's Guards at the Tower of London

Right Tower Bridge

the first day in London, we bought six days' worth of London Pass with Tubes and rail access. The Tube is another name for the London Underground Rail System. It is like the New York City Subway or Washington DC metro rail. I looked at the London Pass itinerary, and I was glad that I packed my workout shoes. It would be a race against time to visit even half of the tourist spots listed in the London Pass in six days. A London Pass gives access to over ninety attractions in and around London. The ticket price of the attractions included in the London Pass was substantially lower than the individual regular tickets. We would have to visit fifteen attractions each of the six days, to see all ninety attractions listed in the London Pass guide. In the next six days, we ran in and out of London by Tube, train, taxi, and Uber for six days absorbing British royalty and the London lifestyle. In the end, we visited only about twenty places. The lazy traveler in me could not be lazy on this trip. However, it was a very exciting and memorable week with a gang of sisters-in-law and brothers-in-law.

Air travel has brought the

world closer than ever. However, the complicated system gets out of gear without much warning. There was chaos at the gate at Kennedy Airport in New York. By 8:15 pm, the boarding time, about 300 passengers had arrived at the boarding gate to board the plane. All those passengers were milling around in a small space near the boarding gate for the Virgin Atlantic flight to London Heathrow Airport (LHR). Occasionally, I heard announcements meant to tell us that Virgin Atlantic apologized for the delay. The reason for the delay was that the plane from London Heathrow Airport was late. The 9:30 pm departure finally happened at 11: 00 PM. When we were airborne, I thought I would catch some sleep. No such luck. Whenever I tried to shut my eyes, the lights came on in full brightness, and all kinds of commotion began. At 12 am, they started serving dinner. I skipped dinner and tried to get some shuteye. Harsh lights came on again at 4:30 am, and it was time for breakfast. I heard instructions to fasten seat belts for bumpy rides in between numerous sounds, bells, and beeps. The flight arrived at LHR at 10:45 am instead of 9:30 am. We arrived late by an hour, which was not too bad.

We left the baggage area, and I saw the sign for SIM Local, a phone store. A reviewer on TripAdvisor wrote about that store. He also discussed the types of SIM cards with prices appropriate for UK travel. Our US-based cell service would not work in the UK. The store SIM Local was in Terminal 2, just outside the security, on Level 1. We bought two local "3 " brand SIM cards for 25 pounds each, as planned. The total cost with taxes was 66 dollars for the two cards. We had 100 minutes of talk, 1000 texts, and 1 gigabyte of data. To my pleasant surprise, it just took about 10 minutes to complete the transaction, and we were talking and texting using our phones. All we needed was a credit card. The cell phone business in England and Europe is like in India – small and big cell phone stores, both chain and individual, are all over the city. I saw at least one at every Tube Station, in our hotel, and in a convenience store. The difference with India is the absence of document requirements and a complicated approval process.

Her Highness (my wife) and I were still in Terminal 2. When the phone was activated, Her Highness called her big sister. She was on a train from New Castle to London. The two sisters got busy with long conversations. The $66 for one week was a little high for the phone plan. The ability to start talking to the sister as soon as possible was priceless.

We got our phones, talked, and had breakfast in an airport cafe. It was time for our hotel transfer. I saw two young women seated behind a table, under a sign displaying a big "I." I assumed the "I" was for information. It was the information desk. I told them my hotel name and asked how to get there. They told me that the Tube would be the fastest and cheapest. However, there were stairs in some stations; navigation with bags might be a problem. I was too tired to drag the bags up and down the stairs. So, I asked for other options. They suggested a private cab instead of a meter taxi. The private cab was at a fixed rate of £54 and would take about an hour to go to the hotel. The regular cab would turn the meter on and could even cost up to £70. At the information desk, one of the young ladies handed me a card with a toll-free number for the car company and pointed her finger to the pay phone. The number worked at the pay phone, a free call, and I hired a private cab. The dispatcher told me that the driver would come inside the terminal. The dispatcher also told me the driver would have a cardboard sign with my name.

President Hotel Entrance

The car appeared in about 20 minutes.

I saw a gentleman approaching with a cardboard sign. And what do you know - my name was written right on that board in big letters. He had to park his car in a designated area about ten minutes away. He helped us with the luggage cart and loaded the bags into the vehicle. We were on our way to Russel Square Station in Central London. At President Hotel, I paid for the car with a credit card. The credit card payment cost us an additional £2 in fees. I decided to save my cash for the time being. I was pleasantly surprised by how smoothly the transfer happened.

Later I learned that taking the Tube from Heathrow would not require dragging our suitcases up any stairs. There were direct trains between Heathrow and Russel Square Station. Russel Square Station had elevators, and the hotel was only 2 to 3 minutes away. Later I noticed guests walking in with big bags from Russel Square station to the hotel. At the airport, after the sleepless night in the aircraft, the Tube trip seemed worse than it was. So, I thought I would take the Tube on our way back to Heathrow and save time and big bucks. Unfortunately, no such luck. We had to leave the hotel by 6 am on Sunday, September 11. However, the train on the Piccadilly line starts at 7 am on Sundays.

On September 3, 2016, the brothers and sisters-in-law settled in President Hotel. Two sisters bought London Pass for

St Pancras Railway Station, London

six days for £109 each and a 7-day Oyster card for £44 each. The Oyster card is a prepaid train pass. They purchased them online in the USA before departure to London. The other two sisters and I did not have London Pass or train pass. The London Pass advertised that visiting three exhibits a day would pay for the price of a three-day pass. The pass will be active on the first day of travel. After the evening tea, on the first day in London, we decided to walk to Kings Cross station to buy our London and train pass. The station was about a mile away from the hotel. The Office of Transportation for London Information at Kings Cross sold London passes and Oyster cards.

We left our hotel and started our walk to the north on Guilford Street. Our hotel was in Guilford. We turned left on Grays Inn Road towards Euston Road and walked into the station area at the end of the Grays Inn. We entered the new concourse building, located the Transportation for London Information, and bought our passes and tickets. The visit to Kings Cross and back on a leisurely pace was wonderful. I did not have a chance to do that leisurely walk again during our week in London. Starting the next day, the pace of our activities was fast and furious.

I liked the Tube and thought it would be worth mentioning a few interesting tidbits. London Tube is the equivalent of the subway system of New York. The Tube is much easier to use, cleaner, and easier to navigate with the help of the escalators and elevators. The stations are well-lit and brighter than those in NY or Washington. I did not get any foul smell in any of the stations I had been to. There were smiling faces (ok, not everyone) of Tube workers ready and willing to help the lazy traveler like me. I saw them guiding the passengers at ticket counters, turnstiles, near elevators and escalators, and outside the busy stations during rush hours.

One Tube worker was posted on the sidewalk near the

entrance of Russel Square Station at rush hour and directed the passengers to the gates or tracks. I saw Tube workers quickly taking positions near the train car doors when a train entered the station and stopped at the platform. They helped the passengers to get in and out of the train. The trains were clean, well-maintained, and frequent. The first time inside a station, I saw a sign reading, "Please mind the gap between the train and the platform," and heard a warning on the public address system. I was wondering what that gap was! It was the gap between the platform edge and the train floor's edge at the entrance door. There were significant gaps horizontally and vertically at some platforms. The gaps must be 4 to 6 inches at some stations. These gaps appeared when Transport for London introduced the new trains. Some of the old platforms did not precisely match the height of the new trains.

We had a complimentary English breakfast in the hotel every morning at Saracen Carvery. This was the restaurant at the Lobby level of the President Hotel. We learned an interesting story about breakfast served in that hotel. Full English breakfast included fried egg, sausage, porridge, bacon, baked beans, hash brown, toast, half-roasted tomato, coffee, tea, and juice. After three days of precisely the same menu, I asked a dressed-up waiter when they would change the menu. He told me they had the same menu for the last ten years, and he did not think it would ever change. The waiters and the managers were all Bangladeshi, and everyone was from Sylhet District (now Division) of Bangladesh. After the first day, they knew all of us. They used to reserve a corner table for seven every morning. They also helped us find Sylheti fish curry restaurant.

Starting September 4, for the next six days, at about 10 am, the group assembled in the lobby and marched to the Tube station like seven ducks. The day's program was pre-planned or prepared on the fly. The program was passed on to the group at the breakfast table. Every day. And every day we walked, took the train and visited the attractions until lunchtime. We took a lunch break for about an hour and repeated the walking and riding routine in the afternoon. We went back to the hotel between 5:30 and 6:30 pm. By about 7:30, we were out to hunt for a London food experience. We repeated the same routine for six days except for Friday. That day we took a bus to visit Stratford upon Avon, about two hours away from London. That, of course, was the birthplace of William Shakespeare. That day we went out by 7 am to get to the tour bus and had a brown bag breakfast on the bus.

Monday, September 5, we visited the Tower of London. It was also the first day of using the London Pass. We had one-day unlimited access to a hop-on hop-off bus tour included in the London Pass. We used this bus tour to travel to the Tower of London. The Golden Tour's double-decker bus took us through the city neighborhoods, shopping districts, and tourist spots. There was dropping off and picking up passengers on its way. That morning the rain stopped, and the neighborhoods and retail businesses on our path looked beautiful from the top of the double-decker bus. We disembarked at the Tower of London stop. It took us about an hour to get there from our hotel.

The Tower of London was built as a fortress to keep the local enemies away and to watch for approaching enemies on the Thames River. Over the years, the Tower of London was used for various purposes, including prison. It is the oldest fortress, palace, and prison in Europe. These days the Tower contains an enormous collection of historic armaments and armor,

Tower Bridge, London

including three coronation swords. One of the most popular attractions of the Tower was the crown jewels.

The Tower of London was one of the most infamous prisons. In this castle, many famous executions were carried out. During the reign of Henry VIII, many thousands were executed in the Tower. Two of Henry's six wives, Anne Boleyn and Katherine Howard, also were executed at the Tower. Anne Boleyn was the second wife, and Katherine Howard was the fifth wife. Anne Boleyn was accused of treason because she could not produce a desired male heir for Henry. Katherine Howard was charged with treason for committing adultery. They were both beheaded at the Tower.

The most important jewel of interest to us was the Koh-i-Noor. Growing up in India, we read about the Mayur Shingasan (the Peacock Throne) and the Koh-i-Noor in elementary and middle school history books. The literal meaning of Koh-i-Noor is Mountain of Light. This was one of the largest diamonds in the world. The Koh-i-Noor was a part of the Mayur Shingasan. There were many stories about the Mayur Shingasan. The Koh-i-Noor and the Akbar Shah Diamond, another famous Mughal treasure piece, formed the peacock's eyes on the Mayur Shingasan. Mughal emperor Shah Jahan inaugurated the Mayur Shinghsan in his court in the Red Fort.

The Akbar Shah Diamond changed hands many times. It was a rough stone. It is believed that the stone was polished and given a different shape. The last known owner of the stone is believed to be the Gaekwad dynasty of Baroda, India.

In 1739, Nadir Shah invaded India, defeated the Mughals, and took the throne to Persia. Later, when the British brought Persia and India under British colonial rule, they took the Koh-i-Noor diamond to Britain. Recently some Indian NGOs (Non-Governmental Organizations) brought legal action in India to force Britain to return the Koh-i-Noor to India. Some groups in Pakistan, Afghanistan, and Iran also made similar efforts. These

Queen Mary's Crown

Torture at the Tower

Tower of London

legal and non-governmental actions are hanging at different stages in four countries. Britain claims that the Koh-i-Noor was obtained under a legitimate treaty. As per British claim, Ranjit Singh's son Maharaja Duleep Singh presented the diamond to Queen Victoria. However, Duleep was only eleven years old and considered a minor. In any case, at present, the Koh-i-Noor is a part of Queen Elizabeth's crown. It was on display in the Tower of London.

We swiped our London Pass at the Tower of London gate and walked toward the Tower building right before us. Just inside the entrance gate and on our right side, I noticed a sign saying "Torture at the Tower." It was on the side of a walkway leading to a narrow door that opened to a narrow stair going down. There were three rooms full of replicas of original torture devices on display. There was this device named the Rack. The Rack was like a platform. The prisoner is laid on the Rack, and his arms and legs are tied with one end of a rope. The other end of the rope went around a pulley. The pulley turned with a lever to tighten and stretch the rope until the arm and leg joints of the prisoner were dislocated, or the prisoner confessed.

We stopped at the Tower of London entrance to see the three guards, the Queen's Guards. They were on duty and, as usual, were standing absolutely still. During the few minutes we were there, I did not see any guard even blinking his eye. The tall, black, fuzzy hat and the red tunic make the guards look cute and more like actors than fighters. In practice, they are the queen's bodyguards, and I was told they would not hesitate to get into fighting mode if required. The hat is about eighteen inches high and made out of the skin of a whole black bear. And no wonder it is called bearskin. We heard one of the guards shouting very loud and sharp commands when a young visitor was too close to a guard.

Inside the Tower, we saw the coronation swords and spoons.

Then we quickly passed by the armaments and the armors. We headed to the crown jewels through a hall full of royal jewelry. We were looking around for the crowns. Then at the end of the hall, we noticed a sign saying the Crown Jewels. The crowns were placed inside a glass case on a long table in the middle of the room. On two sides of the table, two one-way moving walkways were carrying visitors on both sides of the table, allowing quick viewing of the crowns. Two elevated platforms were close to the left and right walls for leisurely viewing. The British royals did not like the visitors to stick too close to the crowns for too long. In addition, photography was strictly prohibited.

We quickly stepped on the moving walkway and were dumped on the other side. There were six crowns on the table, and Queen Victoria's crown with Koh-i-Noor was the last one. I was unhappy with the quick viewing. I went on to the viewing platform for more prolonged observation. I looked at the glittering piece of stone, and my love for the land of my birth, India, overtook me. The British Monarchs had ruled India for over two hundred years. Koh-i-Noor is one of the treasures that the British monarchs acquired from India.

Torture at the Tower

It is a common feeling of many Indians that this diamond should have been in the National Museum in Delhi. I am so close to it ... I can break the glass, grab the stone, run away, get lost in the crowd, and then hand over the stone to the Prime Minister of India, Mr.Modi. I saw the Bharat Ratna award being slipped on my neck. That thought brought goosebumps the size of a marble on my skin. Or maybe, I had hives. Did I take my allergy pill that morning? In any case, some energy started flowing down my body. My biceps bulged out, and I flexed my arms like a bodybuilder I saw in a TV show. My toes felt thicker and stronger inside the sneakers as if they would burst out. I raised myself on my toes, and it seemed I could float in the air.

I heard a voice saying, "Jump! Do not waste time! Get the stone and run."

I tried one more time to flex my toes. I felt so light that I thought I could touch the roof. Then I bent my body like a diver on a diving board and jumped forward. I landed on the moving walkway, jumped up, and grabbed the glass case with my arms around it. I kicked the people on the walkway, planted myself firmly on the side of the table like a lizard, and started pounding on the glass case. What the heck.... the glass should break or at least crack. Then I tried to dislodge the glass case—I started to shake and pull the case. Right at that moment, I heard the clacking sound of heels. I thought, finally, the glass case was cracking. Then I looked to my right—Oh no.! Three short, red-dressed, black tall-headed palace guards are running toward me. Two of them grabbed my arms; the third put his arms on my shoulder and pulled me down. The three fuzzy-hat red guards started to drag me to a door on the left. Hey—where did that door come from? There was no door there! I began to scream at the top of my voice. The door opened to a yard. The yard looked familiar. That was the front of the Tower. The yard was empty. Hundreds of people filled the yard when we came in. Not a single person I could see now.

The three red Brits almost lifted me off the ground and ran to a door on the wall. I saw the sign that said 'Torture at the

Model of a Torture Rack, Tower of London

Tower.' Now I know where they are taking me—I saw those torture machines. I thought those machines were old and did not look too strong. But those three red shorties are strong enough to mangle my body. I tried to flex my biceps and toes. They did not do a thing—what a betrayal! We were almost near the door, and I was desperate—I started to scream again at the top of my voice. Where were Her Highness, the sisters, and the brothers-in-law?

Next, I started threatening, 'I am an American citizen. I want to see the US ambassador.'

The red shorty on my right started laughing, 'You are a petty thief and troublemaker—no ambassador will come near you.'

'If you do not let me go, Obama will send a bunch of marines. Do you know the Marines? The tall guys with big guns? You do not even have a gun. They will kick the hell out of you.'

All three were laughing and pushing me through the torture chamber door. At the bottom of the stairs, the exhibition hall was empty. Where were all the visitors? Where were those rusted machines? The hall had been packed with people milling around the dilapidated, no-good torture machines.

The guards turned right and entered an almost dark room. That room, like a dungeon, was not there when we came here earlier. A giant contraption is in front of us, with two huge rectangular metal planks set up like jaws. This machine looked well-oiled and in top shape. The guards threw me on the bottom plank, and another guard started cranking a pulley. The top plank began to descend on me. I rolled on my side to slip out of the plank. One of the guards kicked me on the back and pushed me to the middle of the plank. The top plank almost touched my nose, and I felt my nose burning. I lifted my arms in an attempt to push the top plank up. I quickly brought them down on my sides. It was too hot. I gave up all hope and was waiting to die.

Did I hear it right? Was not that Her Highness's voice? Yelling at me!

'Shunchho (are you listening?), this is not your nap time. We just took a short break.'

That was Her Highness! I jumped up and was so happy to see the Tower Bridge in front of me. I was sitting on a park bench on the Thames. I turned my head and saw Her Highness walking with the rest of the group. They were walking in the east direction under the Tower Bridge.

Torture at the Tower

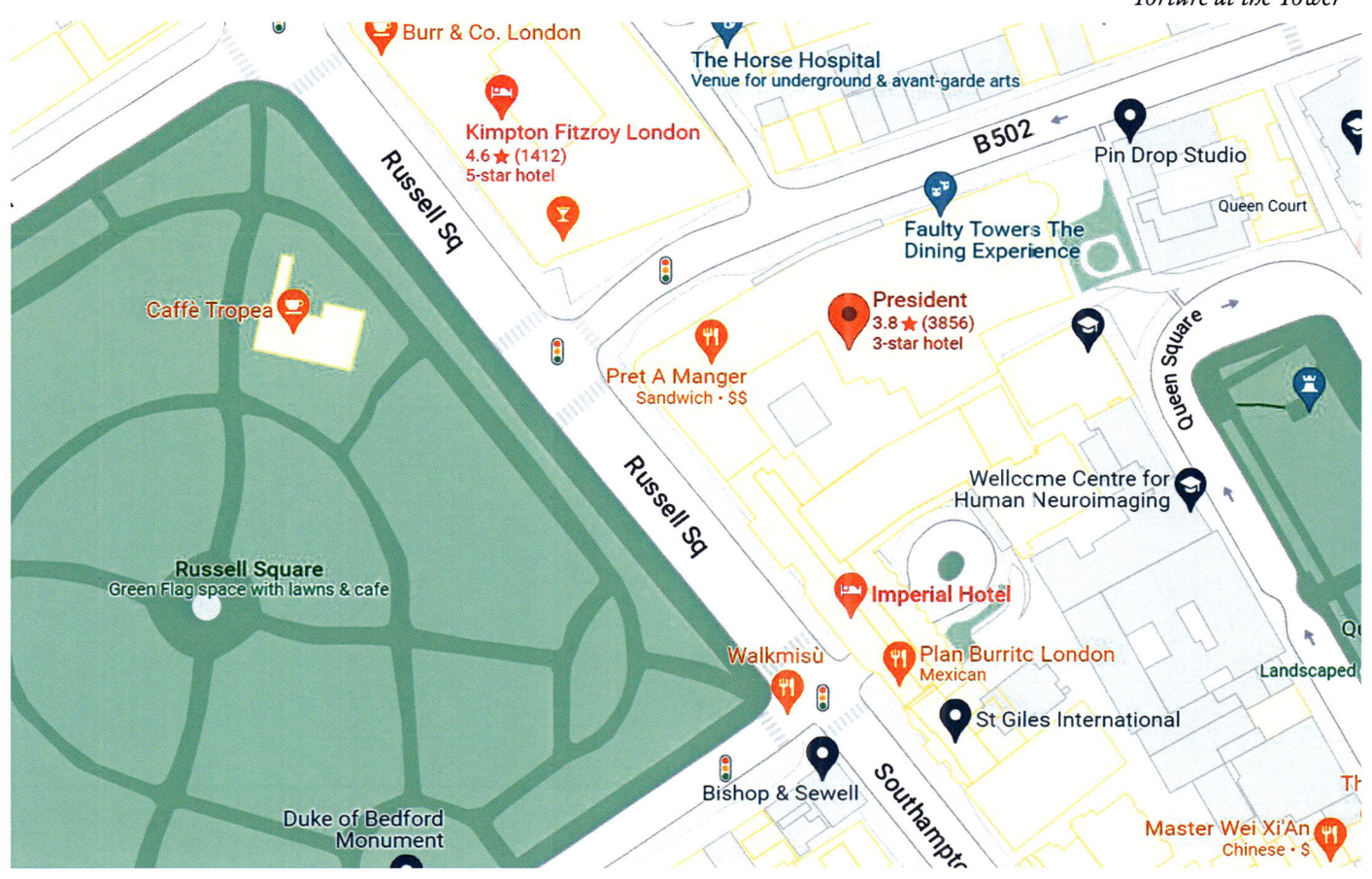

Top *The President Hotel, Russell Square, London*

Bottom *The Tower Of London, London*

56

Dabbawal upon Tyne

We were walking in the Eldon Square Shopping Center in Newcastle upon Tyne. A city on the northeastern coast of England, about three hundred miles from London. We were watching the shoppers, shops and many little people. The little people were in strollers, on foot, and on Dad's shoulder. We saw the big store in the mall, Marks and Spencer. The MS was like Macy's in America. Unlike Macy's, the MS has a restaurant and a grocery store in the same building on the basement level.

Top Dabbawalla's bicycle

Left Dabbawal's Display dabbas

Some of the same American shopping world casts of characters, like Levi's, Clark's, and Claire's, were also present on this side of the pond called the Atlantic. The shoppers looked like the shoppers back home, in the good old USA. They were eating and drinking, looking for bargains, buying, and talking a lot on the phone.

We went shopping for a few hours. Shopping is not an easy chore, add the deep sociological observations in the mix, and there was the perfect storm in the appetite department. Our host was a food lover and was ready for the challenge. We were not after a big feast. Gastronomical adventures were in our minds. Our fearless host took the lead and gave us the marching order.

We walked to Grey Street, around the Grey's Monument, and down towards the Tyne River. Charles Grey, 2nd Earl Grey, was from New Castle and was the Prime Minister of England from 1830 to 1834. He passed the Great Reform Act of 1832. The Great Reform Act changed the electoral process and added many more voters from different social and economic statuses. The Grey's monument commemorated the

Lazy Traveler's City Walk

Left top   Eldon Square, Newcastle upon Tyne, England

Left bottom   Greys Monument, Newcastle upon Tyne, England

Right   Dabbawal Street Food Kitchen, 69-75-High-Bridge, Newcastle upon Tyne, England

Great Reform Act of 1832. The Grey Street and Grey's monument were named after Charles Grey, 2nd Earl Grey. The Earl Grey tea also was named after him.

Grey Street ran down to Mosley Street and then became Dean Street. We did not have to go too far with our growling stomachs. After a few blocks, one left turn, and a walk of a few hundred yards, we were in front of the restaurant named Dabbawal Street Food Kitchen at 69-75 High Bridge. The Dabbawal name and the food idea were inspired by the Dabbawalas of Mumbai, India.

The Dabbawalas are all over Mumbai, India. They deliver fresh home-cooked food to the Mumbai office workers in Dabbas. The literal translation of the Hindi word dabba is a box. The literal translation of the word Dabbawala is a person who carries a box. They are on a bike, on foot, and on the train, moving any which way in the city. They carry the dabbas, the multi-container round Indian-style lunch boxes locally called a

Dabbawal upon Tyne

tiffin carrier. These boxes are usually made of stainless steel, have a six- to four-inch diameter, and are three to four inches high. Three or four are stacked, one on top of the other. The height of the stacked boxes is about twelve inches. The boxes slide into a frame with a carrying handle at the top. What are the contents of the dabbas? The mouthwatering contents of the dabbas are at the core of this story. About five thousand Dabbawalas are scurrying about

Left top Dabbawala on bike

Left bottom   Mumbai Dabbawala on foot

Right top   Dabbawala with pushcart

in Mumbai to deliver the dabbas to the hungry office workers at lunchtime.

A four or five-box dabba will contain four or five home-cooked Indian food items. At lunchtime, boxes are removed from the frame and placed on the office lunchroom table. The contents include a few rotis, a cup of rice, a vegetable curry, dal, and a simple salad with a few green chilies. These items would be neatly placed in each box of the dabba. A non-vegetarian menu dabba will contain meat, fish, or egg curry. A roti is a handmade flat thin bread like a tortilla, a staple for people of the Western and Northern parts of India.

On the other hand, rice is a staple for the people of Eastern and Southern parts of India. Many Indians eat both roti and rice for main meals, lunch, and dinner. In this story, the dal refers to cooked dried pulses like lentils and gram. The cooked dal looks and tastes like spicy soup.

The Dabbawalas start working at half past nine in the morning. They pick up the dabbas from the homes, flats, hundreds of rental buildings, and food suppliers and rush them to the office workers. These workers live far from the city, and the commute takes about three hours on average. The commuters get out of their home by eight in the morning. Homemakers, mostly, or family members do the shopping and

cooking. The cooked food is placed in the dabbas, and the dabbas are placed outside the apartment door, house door, at a designated spot, or handed over to the Dabbawala. The dabbas were delivered to the right person between 11 AM and 12 PM. A customer pays 600 to 1000 Indian Rupees per month for the service. The food in the dabbas stays fresh for about five hours. The dabbas are placed inside insulated bags to maintain proper temperatures. The collection of empty dabbas starts at 1:30 PM, and they are returned to the owners by 4 PM.

The Dabbawalas, primarily men, are dressed in a white shirt, white Dhoti, or pants with a white cap. They are part of a five thousand-member strong group known as the Dabbawalas of Mumbai. A dhoti is a piece of rectangular cloth, usually white in color, worn by Hindu males. The Dhoti is warped around the waist and covers both legs. It looks somewhat like baggy pants. The Dabbawalas usually carry an identity card with them. They are famous for being appropriately dressed and punctual. Their salary is about 8000 Indian rupees (about $150) a month. The Dabbawalas lack literacy. Their average education level is eighth grade. They use a complex coding system based on color and symbols to manage

the collection and delivery of the dabbas. The codes are inscribed on top of each dabba.

The so-called first and last miles are usually traveled by bike or foot. They do not use motorized vehicles, not even motorcycles. Motorized vehicles are subject to malfunction and traffic stops. In addition, most of these vehicles must follow the one-way rules strictly. Bikes and pushcarts are exempted from strict traffic rules. If there is a traffic jam, bikes and carts can easily navigate out of the jam.

Left   Dabbawal's Water Tank

Right top Dabbawal's Chicken & Bhelpuri, Dabbawal's Dosa.

Right bottom Dabbawala's Dabba

The dabbas are collected from the homes or apartments and carried on foot or by bike to a collection place. The dabbas are loaded on pushcarts and pushed to the nearest local train station. In some commuter trains, there are designated compartments for the Dabbawalas, usually the last compartment of the train. The dabbas are placed on flat wooden crates at the station, with up to one hundred fifty dabbas each. These crates are then loaded into the train compartment. The loading into the train compartment and unloading at the designated station need special skills, coordination, and agility. The trains and the platforms are usually crowded. The transfers are generally done in less than a minute. The trains typically stop for about a minute at the stations. The lack of education

did not prevent the Dabbawalas from delivering on time to the correct office and person. Missing lunch delivery is a rare incident. The Dabbawalas claim that they are Six Sigma certified and are subject to study at many business schools worldwide. One criterion of being Six Sigma certified is that the likelihood of error will be 3.4 per million deliveries.

The Dabbawalas are the inspiration for this eatery; we were in the Dabbawal. We liked the pleasing ambiance when we stepped into the restaurant. The decorations reminded us of the great Dabbawala profession of Mumbai, India. We saw a few dabbas and a model bike on a shelf. Graphics depict the hurrying Dabbawalas on the exterior windows and door glass. There were just enough trade tools and graphics samples to describe Dabbawalas's profession.

The bathroom inside the eatery was clean and modern with an interesting twist. It had a cast iron overhead water tank with a pull chain, not one of those lower-level modern water closets with turn leaver. The bathroom reminded me of the bathrooms of years back in India, with a cast iron-pull-chain water tank. The tank was a British import to India. It became an Indian tradition, and the sight took me back to 1960s India.

The Dabbawal served various portions of chaat and finger foods as snacks or starters. These were popular Indian street food served in a pleasing indoor eating arrangement. Many medium and large full meals

Top Contents of a Dabbawala's dabba

Right So Long Dabbawal

were also in the offerings. We had bhelpuri, samosa, dosa, onion palak bhajis, and grilled chicken. The chaat, dosa, and chicken made everyone happy except me on the table. I was craving panipuri. There was none on the menu. The picture of Bombay Bomb looked like panipuri, which I ordered, and we ate. Dessert was not in the plan at Dabbwal. That would have been a stop by itself at the Royal Sweets. We had to order pistachio kulfi to smooth out the Bombay Bomb spicy taste from our taste buds.

Dabbawal claimed their clients would have an authentic Mumbai street food experience. I thought it was not too close to the street food experience. The food was delicious. The ambiance was pleasing and interesting. And who has a street food stomach anymore? Please raise your hand and say yea. All in all, it was a lovely gastronomical event for a lazy traveler like me. So long, Dabbawal.

Lazy Traveler's City Walk

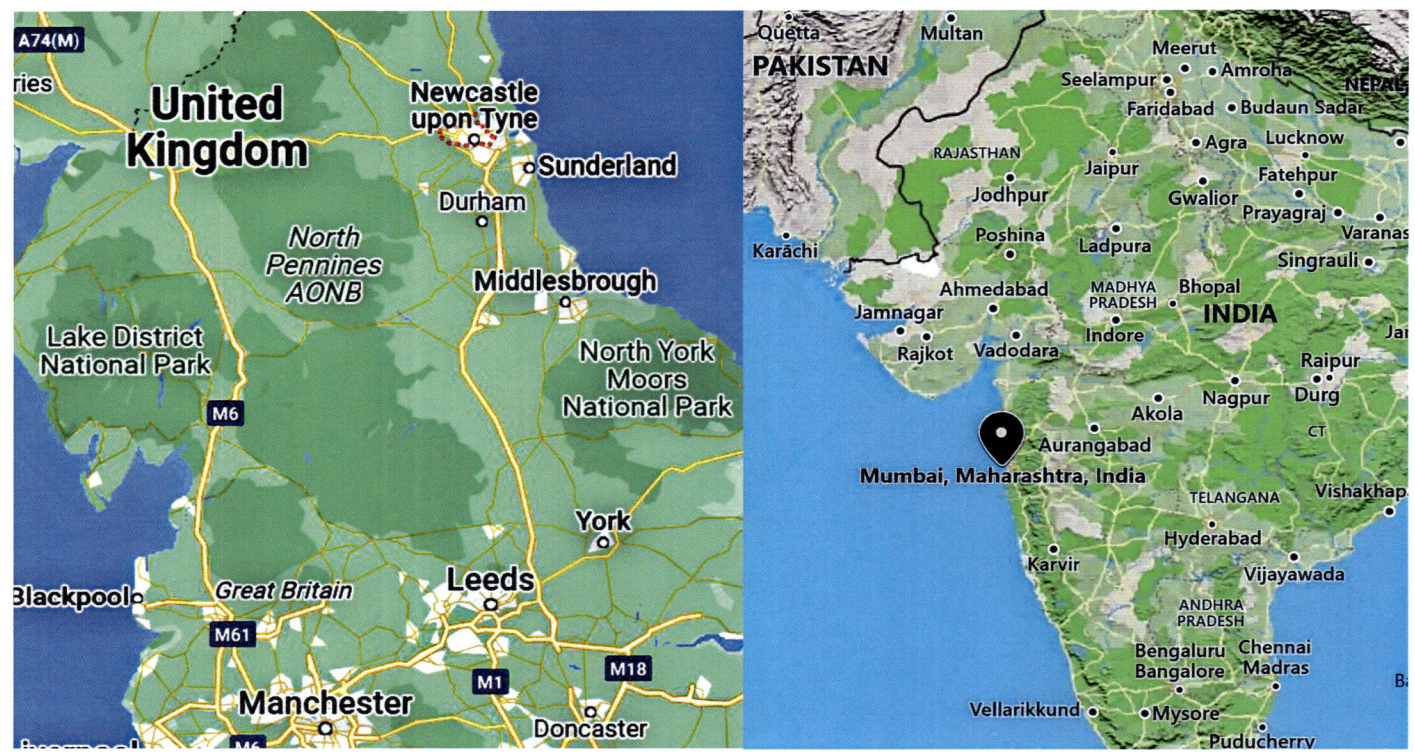

Top Newcastle upon Tyne,   Right Mumbai India,   Below Marks & Spencer to Dabbawal, Newcastle, England

Dabbawal upon Tyne

Roadometer to Odometer

Our bus stopped at the National Oregon/California Trail Center in Montpelier, Idaho. This stop was unscheduled and was a surprise. It was the last full day of our escorted bus tour across the Mountain Standard Time Zone. I was so happy that the visit happened. Inside the Trail Center, I saw something I had never seen before or expected to see anytime. It was a roadometer, an early version of an odometer. The pioneers attached a roadometer to a wooden wheel of a trail wagon.

Left Mormon Roadometer attached to a wagon wheel
Top Conestoga Covered Wagon

The roadometer recorded the miles traveled on the wagon.

We were on our way to Salt Lake City from Jackson, Wyoming. Our country is enormous. We must fly, ride, drive, walk, and walk more to see this beautiful country. That was what we were doing. We flew from Washington, DC, to Rapid City, South Dakota. Our bus tour started from Rapid City. We stopped at Mount Rushmore, Crazy Horse Memorial, Cody, Yellowstone National Park, Grand Teton National Park, and Jackson, Wyoming. We ended our travel in Salt Lake City, Utah, after traveling over a thousand miles in a big bus and walking many miles inside the parks. The lazy traveler in me did not get too many chances to be lazy on this trip, except when I was sitting on the bus and looking through the bus window.

The address of the Center is U.S. 89 and 320 North 4th Street in Montpelier, Idaho. It is located on the historic Oregon Trail. The Center brought the story of the pioneers to life. The pioneers first explored the little-known western states like Oregon and California. They left their home, community, and a comfortable and familiar

Left Covered Wagon at the High Desert Museum

Right Gun shop - simulated

country in the eastern states. They traveled to the West to explore new places. The Center presents a simulation of the Oregon and California wagon trail. The pioneers traveled across the wild and isolated American West. Their 2000-mile-long journey began in Missouri in the east and ended in the Oregon territory. The travel to Oregon took about six months. The visitors see a gun shop and a mercantile, then go for a simulated wagon ride and experience the nighttime encampment.

The Oregon Trail ran east to West from Independence, Missouri, to Oregon City, Oregon. It was a 2000-miles long, narrow trail, navigable on foot or horseback. The fur traders and trappers created and used that trail until 1840.

In 1836 the emigrants organized the first wagon train from east of the Missouri River. The pioneer families joined together and formed wagon trains. There were hundreds of wagons in a wagon train. Traveling by a single wagon often experienced terrible consequences. The attacks by the American Indians, side-stepping into wrong trails, and running out of supplies were common situations. Wagon trains were well organized, with elected leaders and a group of deputies. Each train had an experienced trail guide. These guides could recognize the trails created by American Indians or a herd of wild animals. The first train started from Independence, Missouri, and reached Idaho. If a family decided to join a wagon train, it would save money for about five years before the travel time. This family would need $400 for a wagon and $1000 for supplies in 1840s dollars.

Life in a wagon train was orderly and systematic. Before daybreak, blowing a trumpet or rifle firing would wake the pioneers. By 7 am, every family would be in their wagon, and a trumpeter would signal a "Wagons Ho" to start the train onto the trail. From noon to 1 pm, the train would stop for lunch and take care of the animals. The day's travel would end at 5 pm, and by 8 pm, the

pioneers would settle down for the night. The night guards would take their positions. The guards would change at midnight.

The trail was an unpaved, bumpy road. The California trails became prominent in 1849. That year, the rumor about California's gold was spreading like wildfire. The 49ers created many California trails. Thousands of gold prospectors from the eastern part of the United States arrived in California in search of gold in 1949. There were people from South American and European countries, Mexico, and China, who also arrived in California in search of gold in the same year. These prospectors were mainly men and called the 49ers. The trails passed through Missouri, Kansas, Nebraska, Colorado, Wyoming, Idaho, Utah, Nevada, Oregon, and California. In 1978 the U.S. Congress officially named this trail the Oregon National Historic Trail. That naming has helped to preserve three hundred miles of the trail.

The pioneers needed to start their journey in April and reach Oregon by October. After October, the grass that fed the livestock would die, and snow would cover the mountain passes, making them difficult to pass.

Top   Mercantile - simulated

Right   Wagon getting ready for the trail - simulated

Roadometer to Odometer

Why did the pioneers migrate to Oregon and California? The Christian missionaries were the first to use the trail to reach the American Indians. The goal was to enlighten them. The Mormons migrated to Salt Lake City to safely practice their religion. Most of the pioneers emigrated to make their life better. The Oregon Land Act of 1850 created a rush for land grabs. Under that law, every unmarried white citizen would receive 320 acres of land in the

74

designated area free of charge. Every white married couple would receive 640 acres of land in the designated area free of charge. In general, the biggest attraction was the lower land price compared to the states in the east. The migration to California was for a similar reason. The added attraction for California was the gold rush. Between 1840 and 1850, 250,000 gold seekers migrated to California.

The Oregon/California trail journey was physically and emotionally challenging. About one in ten pioneers did not survive. Most died of diseases like dysentery, cholera, smallpox, or flu. People also died from accidents and exhaustion. Many pioneers drowned during dangerous river crossings.

We got off our bus and walked into the trail center. A representative welcomed us and guided us to the first exhibit of the trail simulation. We stepped into the gun shop and learned about the importance of guns for the pioneers. Guns were necessary for hunting for food and protection. Natural predators like wild animals were in abundance. The robbers and cattle thieves were ready to take advantage of the pioneers. In addition, the American Indians were trying to protect their lands from outsiders like the pioneers. There were firearms on display. We saw short and long guns and rifles. In about the year 1840, flintlock rifles and percussion rifles were available. The flintlock used a spark from a flint stone to set off the gunpowder. A hammer would strike a small impact-sensitive explosive in a percussion rifle to set off the gunpowder. Most adult males in a wagon train would carry one or more weapons. The availability determined the choice of weapons. Most adults had firearms, but not everybody was proficient in using weapons. There were injuries and death by improper handling of the guns.

Our next stop was the Mercantile. It was like a general store on the trail. The pioneers picked food, medicine, tools, and clothing from the store. Below is an estimate of supplies needed for a family of four for about six months of travel. National Oregon/California Trail Center presented that estimate on their web page at https://oregontrailcenter.org/supplies.

"To survive the long journey, a family of four would need 600 lbs. of flour, 120 lbs. of biscuits, 400 lbs. of bacon, 60 lbs. of coffee, 4 lbs. of tea, 100 lbs. of sugar, and 200 lbs. of lard. These would just be the basic staples. Other foodstuffs could include sacks of rice and beans, plus dried peaches, and apples. Bacon was often held in large barrels packed in bran so the hot sun

Left A nighttime encampment, wagons parked in a circle

Right A docent describing the evening activities in an encampment

would not melt the fat. Each man took a rifle or shotgun, and some added a pistol. A good hunting knife was essential. Farm implements include a plow, shovel, scythe, rake, hoe, and carpentry tools like a saw, broad ax, mallet, and plane. The pioneers also carried seeds for corn, wheat, and other crops."

Our next stop was the Wagon train ride. We got into the wagon from the back end and sat on the two long benches on two sides. The docent closed the rear flaps. The wagon started swaying side to side, lurching, and rolling with wheels squeaking. When it stopped, we exited the wagon in a low-light hall. This was a scene depicting an encampment. The day's travel usually ended before dusk, and the pioneers parked the wagons in a circle. They kept the cattle inside the circular perimeter to protect them from thieves and prevent them from running away. This end-of-the-day, temporary living arrangement was called encampment. The docent narrated the usual happenings around the encampment in the evening.

I noticed some gears attached to a wheel of the wagon on display. The docent explained that it was a roadometer. The pioneers attached a wooden roadometer to the rear wheel of the wagon to monitor progress. The pioneers must know how fast they were moving. That helped them to plan for the supplies like water, food, and fuel. In a day, a wagon could travel about 12 miles. They must also mark the location of the graves of their loved ones.

Brigham Young was a Mormon Church leader in the middle of the 19th century. In Illinois, the Mormons were persecuted for their religious practices. Brigham Young organized his followers and emigrated to Salt Lake City in 1847. That was the beginning of Mormon emigration to the West.

In the spring of 1847, a Mormon wagon train started to the West under the leadership of Bingham Young. There were about 3000 families in 2500 wagons on the wagon train. As the wagon train started moving on the trail, Brigham Young asked John Clayton, a fellow pioneer, to monitor the distance traveled in a day.

John Clayton adopted a simple technique. He tied a piece of cloth to the spoke of a wagon wheel and counted the number of revolutions. Then he multiplied the number of revolutions by the length of the wheel's circumference to get the distance traveled. However, one person would have to count the revolutions all day long. The pioneers were looking for a better solution. John Clayton and two fellow pioneers designed a wooden roadometer in 1847. The roadometer recorded the miles traveled each day. Modern vehicles have similar instruments called an odometer to monitor the distance traveled. The odometer is not attached to the wheel of the vehicle directly. It is attached to the engine under the hood to monitor the distance traveled. The wooden Mormon roadometer contributed to the development of the modern-day odometer.

After the simulated trail visit, I came out and sat on a bench in the front hall. I was thinking about the pioneers. They left their home, family, and community and struggled for thousands of miles. They risked their own life and the life of their loved ones. They reached the promised land, enriched their life, expanded the country's horizon, and opened opportunities for others. The thought of the modern pioneers came to my mind. The modern-day pioneers also left their family, friends, community, and comfort of familiarity: thousands of miles away. They

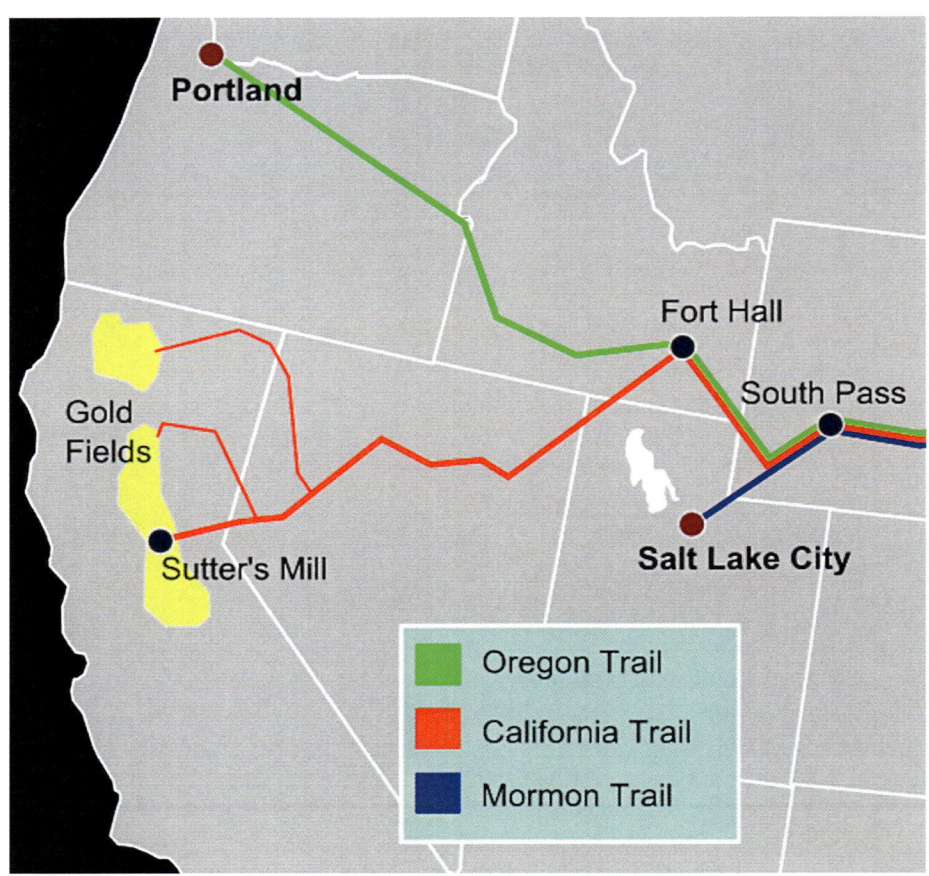

Oregon, California, and Mormon Trail

did not have to ride a wagon on dangerous trails. However, the obstacles were comparable on many levels. These modern-day pioneers added colors and enriched life on both sides of the ocean. I thought it would be an excellent time to pay tribute to the pioneers. Thank you for your sacrifice.

Lazy Traveler's City Walk – Image Attributions and Copyright Information

Book Cover
trip-concept-illustration-3369736
Attribution : Designed by slidesgo / Freepik

Title Page
Vehicle of Taihoku Municipal Bus 1935 Attributions: Unknown author, Public domain, via Wikimedia Commons

Calcutta Becomes Kolkata

Calcutta Double decker bus
Calcutta Double decker bus Calcutta State Transport Corporation Maniktala Bus Depot - Kolkata 2012-01-23 8634. JPG.
Page URL
https://commons.wikimedia.org/wiki/File:Calcutta_State_Transport_Corporation_Maniktala_Bus_Depot_-_Kolkata_2012-01-23_8634.JPG
Attribution: Biswarup Ganguly, CC BY 3.0 <https://creativecommons.org/licenses/by/3.0>, via Wikimedia Commons

Tram in Kolkata 1193

Page URL: https://commons.wikimedia.org/wiki/File:Tram_in_Kolkata_1193.jpg
File URL: https://upload.wikimedia.org/wikipedia/commons/f/f4/Tram_in_Kolkata_1193.jpg
Attribution: Rameshng, CC BY-SA 3.0 <https://creativecommons.org/licenses/by-sa/3.0>, via Wikimedia Commons

Calcutta Tram (14839390675)

Page URL: https://commons.wikimedia.org/wiki/File:Calcutta_Tram_(14839390675).jpg
https://upload.wikimedia.org/wikipedia/commons/f/f0/Calcutta_Tram_%2814839390675%29.jpg
File URL: Attribution: Paul Hamilton, CC BY-SA 2.0 <https://creativecommons.org/licenses/by-sa/2.0>, via Wikimedia Commons

KolkataTraffic1945.jpg

This file is a work of a U.S. Army soldier or employee, taken or made as part of that person's official duties. As a work of the U.S. federal government, it is in the public domain in the United States.

Barcelona – The Street Lamps

Kolkata Gaslight

KolkataTraffic1945.jpg
This file is a work of a U.S. Army soldier or employee, taken or made as part of that person's official duties. As a work of the U.S. federal government, it is in the public domain in the United States.

Barcelona Street Lamp
Google Map (Banc-fanal_del_passeig_de_Gràcia10google-map)

Casa Milà, general view
Page URL: https://commons.wikimedia.org/wiki/File:Casa_Mil%C3%A0,_general_view.jpg
File URL: https://upload.wikimedia.org/wikipedia/commons/d/de/Casa_Mil%C3%A0%2C_general_view.jpg
Attribution: Thomas Ledl, CC BY-SA 4.0 <https://creativecommons.org/licenses/by-sa/4.0>, via Wikimedia Commons

Barcelona streetlamp stone seats
Google Map (Banc-fanal_del_passeig_de_Gràcia-1-google-map)

Barcelona street lamp firebox
Google Map (Banc-fanal_del_passeig_de_Gràcia-4-google-map)

Juliet of Verona
Statua di Giulietta (atrio esterno) - 2018
Page URL: https://commons.wikimedia.org/wiki/File:Statua_di_Giulietta_(atrio_esterno)_-_2018.jpg
File URL: https://upload.wikimedia.org/wikipedia/commons/a/a9/Statua_di_Giulietta_%28atrio_esterno%29_-_2018.jpg
Attribution: Alessandro Pace, CC BY-SA 4.0 <https://creativecommons.org/licenses/by-sa/4.0>, via Wikimedia Commons

Torture at the-tower
Model of a Torture Rack -Tower of London (8145448881)
Page URL: https://commons.wikimedia.org/wiki/File:Tower_of_London_(8145448881).jpg
File URL: https://upload.wikimedia.org/wikipedia/commons/7/76/Tower_of_London_%288145448881%29.jpg
Attribution: Steve Collis from Melbourne, Australia, CC BY 2.0 <https://creativecommons.org/licenses/by/2.0>, via Wikimedia Commons

President Hotel
Page URL: https://commons.wikimedia.org/wiki/File:President_Hotel.JPG
File Url: https://upload.wikimedia.org/wikipedia/commons/2/2f/President_Hotel.JPG
Attribution: BKP, CC BY-SA 3.0 <https://creativecommons.org/licenses/by-sa/3.0>, via Wikimedia Commons

St Pancras Railway Station London
Page URL: https://commons.wikimedia.org/wiki/File:King%27s_Cross_St._Pancras_aerial_view,_image_6.jpg
File URL: https://upload.wikimedia.org/wikipedia/commons/b/bd/King%27s_Cross_St._Pancras_aerial_view%2C_image_6.jpg
Attribution: Héctor Ochoa 'Robot8A', CC BY-SA 4.0 <https://creativecommons.org/licenses/by-sa/4.0>, via Wikimedia Commons

Queen Mary's Crown
This work is in the public domain in the United States because it was published (or registered with the U.S. Copyright Office) before January 1, 1927.

Tower of London (6086262307)
Page URL: https://commons.wikimedia.org/wiki/File:Tower_of_London_(6086262307).jpg
File URL: https://upload.wikimedia.org/wikipedia/commons/b/b0/Tower_of_London_%286086262307%29.jpg
Attribution: Tony Hisgett from Birmingham, UK, CC BY 2.0 <https://creativecommons.org/licenses/by/2.0>, via Wikimedia Commons

Dabbawal upon Tyne

Dabbawalah Pushcart
Page Url: https://commons.wikimedia.org/wiki/File:Dabbawalah.jpg
File Url: https://upload.wikimedia.org/wikipedia/commons/4/48/Dabbawalah.jpg
Attributions: Ayan Khasnabis, CC BY 2.0 <https://creativecommons.org/licenses/by/2.0>, via Wikimedia Commons
Dabbawalah on-foot

Mumbai Dabbawala or Tiffin Wallahs- 200,000 Tiffin Boxes Delivered Per Day
Page Url: https://commons.wikimedia.org/wiki/File:Mumbai_Dabbawala_or_Tiffin_Wallahs-_200,000_Tiffin_Boxes_Delivered_Per_Day.jpg
File Url: https://upload.wikimedia.org/wikipedia/commons/9/9d/Mumbai_Dabbawala_or_Tiffin_Wallahs-_200%2C000_Tiffin_Boxes_Delivered_Per_Day.jpg
Attribution: Steve Evans from Citizen of the World, CC BY 2.0 <https://creativecommons.org/licenses/by/2.0>, via Wikimedia Commons

Office dabba – contents of a Dabbawalah dabba
Page Ural: https://commons.wikimedia.org/wiki/File:Office_dabba.jpg
File Ural https://upload.wikimedia.org/wikipedia/commons/f/fc/Office_dabba.jpg
Attribution: SumeetPatel34, CC BY-SA 4.0 <https://creativecommons.org/licenses/by-sa/4.0>, via Wikimedia Commons

Dabbawallah bicycle
Page Url: https://commons.wikimedia.org/wiki/File:Dabbawallah_bicycle.jpg
File Url: https://upload.wikimedia.org/wikipedia/commons/9/9c/Dabbawallah_bicycle.jpg
Attribution: Bernard Gagnon, CC BY-SA 4.0 <https://creativecommons.org/licenses/by-sa/4.0>, via Wikimedia Commons

Roadometer to Odometer

Covered Wagon at the High Desert Museum - B.D.'s world from Monroe, Washington, United States
Page URL:
https://commons.wikimedia.org/wiki/File:Covered_wagon_at_the_High_Desert_Museum_Outside.jpg

File URL:
https://upload.wikimedia.org/wikipedia/commons/7/7c/Covered_wagon_at_the_High_Desert_Museum_Outside.jpg
Attribute: B.D.'s world from Monroe, Washington, United States, CC BY-SA 2.0
<https://creativecommons.org/licenses/by-sa/2.0>, via Wikimedia Commons

Conestoga wagon on Oregon Trail - NARA - 286056 - Restoration
Conestoga wagon on Oregon Trail
Page URL: Conestoga wagon on Oregon Trail - NARA - 286056 – Restoration
https://commons.wikimedia.org/wiki/File:Conestoga_wagon_on_Oregon_Trail_-_NARA_-_286056_-_Restoration.jpg
File URL:
https://upload.wikimedia.org/wikipedia/commons/a/a6/Conestoga_wagon_on_Oregon_Trail_-_NARA_-_286056_-_Restoration.jpg
Attribute: National Archives and Records Administration, Public domain, via Wikimedia Commons

Oregon-trail-encampment-15 070338
In an encampment, wagons parked in a circle - FLMB Church Historic Documents,
https://flmbc.org/flmbc-lineage-historical-documents